Through Our Eyes
A Journey Through an Autistic Mind

DAVE RUSSELL

Copyright © 2020 Dave Russell

The right of Dave Russell to be identified as the author of this work has been asserted by him in accordance with the Copyright, Designs and Patents Act, 1988.

All rights reserved. No part of this publication may be reproduced, stored in a retrieval system, or transmitted, in any form or by any means, electronic, mechanical, photocopying, recording or otherwise, without the prior permission of the author.

This book is sold subject to the condition that it shall not, by way of trade or otherwise, be lent, re-sold, hired out or otherwise circulated without the author's prior consent in any form of binding or cover other than that in which it is published and without a similar condition including this condition being imposed on the subsequent purchaser.

ISBN: 978-1-99-959781-8

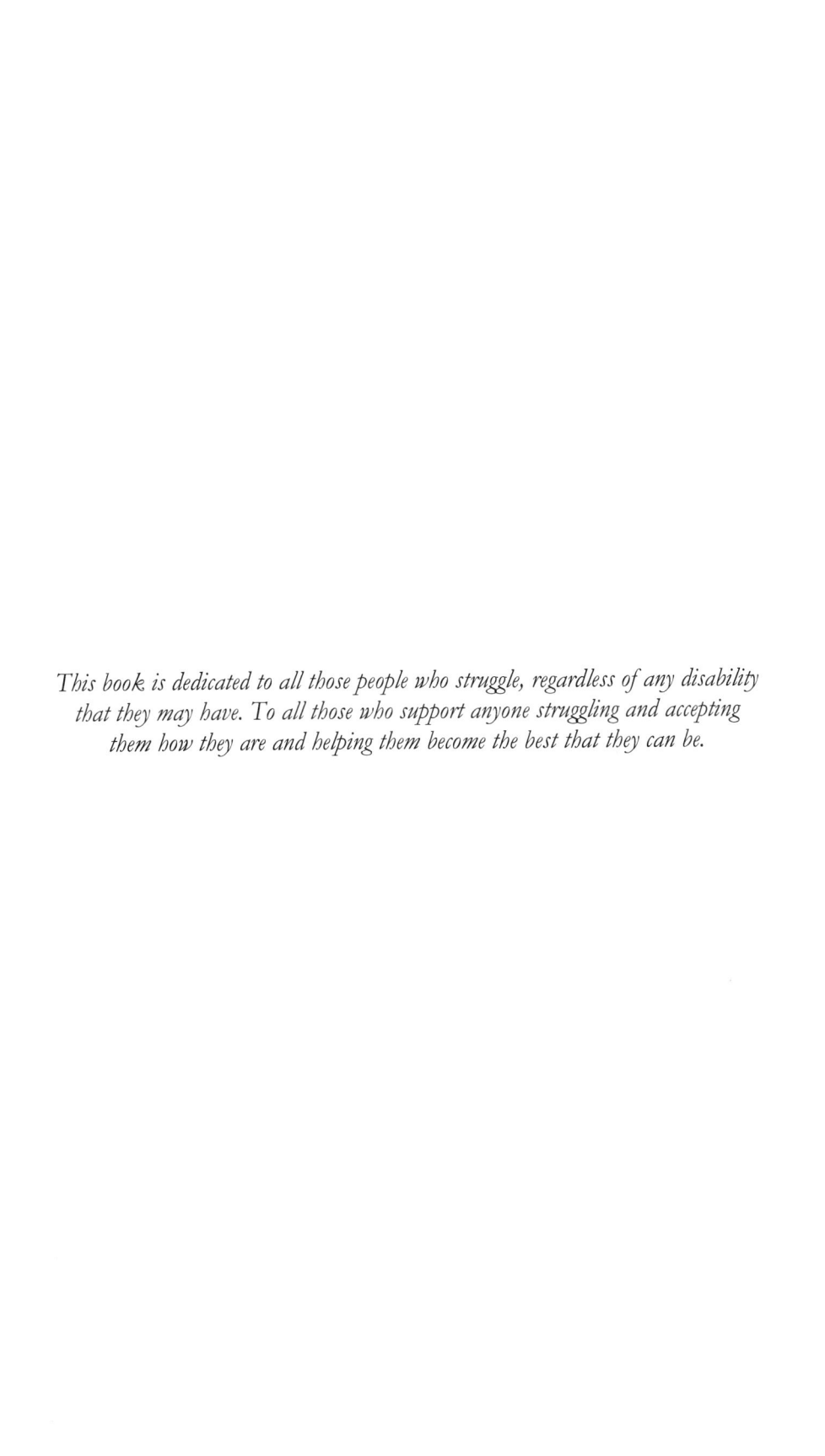

This book is dedicated to all those people who struggle, regardless of any disability that they may have. To all those who support anyone struggling and accepting them how they are and helping them become the best that they can be.

CONTENTS

ACKNOWLEDGMENTS i
INTRODUCTION 1
PERSONAL QUESTIONS 10

    Question 1: Did you ever suspect that you were autistic or had any special needs? 11

    Question 2: Do you prefer to be called an 'autistic person' or 'a person with autism'? Does it really matter? and do you care? 13

    Question 3: Have you always been autistic? You don't look autistic .. 15

    Question 4: Do you ever wonder what it would be like to not be autistic, to be 'normal'? 18

    Question 5: How did you feel when you were told you were autistic? 20

    Question 6: Do you tell people that you are autistic? 22

    Question 7: Do you have any family members that are also autistic? 24

    Question 8: What does autism mean to you? 25

    Question 9: Do you have any other condition aside from autism? 26

    Question 10: Autistic people take things literally, have you ever mistaken your belief or imagination for reality? 27

    Question 11: If there was a cure for autism, would you take it? 28

    Question 12: What feelings do you experience when you are having during one of your extreme highs? 30

    Question 13: Can you describe an extreme low? 31

    Question 14: What would you want to tell someone new who would like to get to know you? 33

    Question 15: Did you enjoy your primary and secondary school? 34

    Question 16: How did you find University? 37

Question 17: Not many autistic people go to University or find it too overwhelming, what would you say to any considering it?...............39

Question 18: Do you have flashback memories?................................41

Question 19: What is the worst thing about being autistic? 42

Question 20: Do you think you would like to be 'normal'? 43

Question 21: How does an autistic person see the world? What do you see first when looking at something? 45

Question 22: Do you have many friends?..46

Question 23: Would you say your primary/secondary school days were good or a bad experience? 47

Question 24: Do you think the school did enough to help and support you? 49

Question 25: How important were your parent(s) help and support? 50

Question 26: Does anyone else in your family have a disability?.......52

Question 27: When was the lowest point in your life and what happened? 53

Question 28: You seem really happy and cheerful, is this an act?......55

Question 29: Outside of either school/work or home, what other support do you have? 56

Question 30: What do you want to do when you leave school/university? What is your ideal career? 57

Question 31: Do you think it is fair that the world believes that you will not be able to do anything and never amount to anything because you're autistic? 58

Question 32: What do you think others need to learn about autistic people like yourself?..60

Question 33: Do people believe that you are autistic when you tell them?...61

Question 34: Do you think that all autistic children should be kept together rather than interacting with other children?......................62

Question 35: Do you feel limited by your disability? 63

Question 36: How are you finding your first job after school / university? 64

Question 37: Why do you obsess over Harry Potter? Do you understand that it is not real? 66

Question 38: What do you think schools / universities can do more to help other autistic students? 67

Question 39: What is the best part of being autistic? 69

Question 40: Do you regularly have panic attacks or meltdowns? 70

Question 41: What makes you happy? 72

Question 42: Do you have any clubs or organisations that you are involved in? 73

Question 43: Being autistic, you must be a Math Genius? 74

Question 44: Do you enjoy your own free time? 75

Question 45: What things does an autistic person enjoy? 76

BEHAVIOURAL QUESTIONS 77

Question 1: Why do you make weird faces all the time? 78

Question 2: Why do you talk so loudly? 80

Question 3: Why do you talk in a weird voice? You sound like a young child? 82

Question 4: Why do you ask the same question over and over again? 84

Question 5: Why do you consistently do things that you are told not to do? 87

Question 6: Why do think people treat autistic people as a child regardless of their age? 89

Question 7: Why does it take you a long time to answer questions? 91

Question 8: Do you avoid having conversations? 93

Question 9: Why do you look bored and avoid eye contact when someone is speaking to you? 95

Question 10: What are you interested in? Autistic people can get very obsessed with something specific. 97

Question 11: Autistic people tend to be more sensitive to different stimulus, are you? 98

Question 12: You seem to react when holding hands with people. Why is that? 100

Question 13: Do you like your own company? 102

Question 14: Why do you not understand body language and facial expressions? 104

Question 15: Do you think your social interactions within a group environment have improved over time? Do you use therapy or learn techniques to help you? 106

Question 16: Do you hate being touched or are there certain areas of your body which are more sensitive to touch? 108

Question 17: Is it true that an autistic person can be really high one minute and then super low the next? 109

Question 18: Why when you make a mistake do you have a meltdown and create such a fuss over nothing? 110

Question 19: Why can you not follow an instruction straight away? 111

Question 20: How do you feel when you are asked or made to do things which are uncomfortable? 113

Question 21: Do you have any strange traits that you do when you are anxious? 114

Question 22: Do you have a good memory and how do you retrieve information you want to recall? 116

Question 23: Are you under or over sensitive to noise? 118

Question 24: Why do you always fidget? Do you have a problem remaining still? 119

Question 25: Why do you do things differently to others? 120

Question 26: Does your over/under sensitivity to noise affect other areas such as pain? 122

Question 27: Why are you extremely picky over food and drink? ...123

Question 28: Are you always very anxious and worry about every single thing? 124

Question 29: Isn't there any medication you can take to stop being autistic most of the time? 125

Question 30: Do you think your ADHD is more manageable with medicine? 126

Question 31: Do you think that your secondary school / university kept you focused enough you stop your disruptive behaviour? 128

Question 32: Is there anything that you constantly struggle with, that you feel that you should not struggle with? 129

Question 33: Why do you interrupt when others are talking? 130

Question 34: Do you think that your behaviour can be inappropriate? 131

Question 35: How do you feel when someone tells you that you are being inappropriate? 132

Question 36: How are you finding secondary school / university? ..133

Question 37: Can you describe what you see and feel when you get anxious? 134

Question 38: Why do you find it difficult to hold someone's hand? 135

Question 39: Is it true that the mental health of an autistic person is more up and down than a non-autistic person? 136

Question 40: What has helped you with your mental wellbeing? 137

Question 41: Do you struggle getting ready in the morning? 138

Question 42: Do you understand the concept of time? 139

Question 43: It is reported that autistic people suffer from sleep disorders, do you? 140

Question 44: Why do you tap your hands and bite your fingernails all the time? 141

Question 45: Why do you always line up toys / items and put them in colour / size order? 142

Question 46: Do you seem to remember and repeat slogans and catchphrases easily? 143

Question 47: You seem to be able to repeat lines in TV shows. Can you repeat whole episodes? 144

Question 48: Do you like reading or do you struggle with the understanding / context of the written piece? 145

Question 49: Why do you get distracted so easily and so often? 146

Question 50: Why do you keep running off? 147

Question 51: Repetition is a key trait for an autistic person. What do you repeat over and over again? 148

Question 52: Do you need cues or prompts to do things or be reminded of the task you have been set? 149

Question 53: Why do you have trouble remaining still, regardless of the situation? 150

Question 54: Is your brain consistently working fast? 152

Question 55: Do you have a detailed timetable for every day and every hour within the day? 153

Conclusion: 154

ABOUT THE AUTHOR 156

ACKNOWLEDGMENTS

This book was an idea and I was not sure I would even get it off the ground to be honest. The interviews every week or so with two of the key members of the group were eye-opening. To all those who went through my questions over email and messages, a long process but I hope you will agree – such a great result.

INTRODUCTION

I embarked on this journey to try and understand how other autistic people see the world and learn about their experiences of how others have seen them. I wanted to know how they managed to deal with the different struggles that they have faced during childhood and into adulthood. This journey turned into one of the biggest eye-opening projects that I have ever completed. I experienced other sides of this condition which were new to me. It showed me how others have struggled and managed to resolve the same issues I, myself, had and how they overcame ones that I have not or could not experience.

During my childhood, I always knew that I saw the world very differently to others – my friends, family, and those in my school. I struggled, and still struggle, in certain social situations despite having been told that I am really good in social settings. I am unable to understand the emotional side that drives people in certain ways. I don't have the empathy that is required to fully understand the situation or event that is taking place. It reminds me of the character, Joy, from the Disney film Inside Out. Spoiler alert – she repeatedly tries to keep Sadness away from the console that controls Riley because she thinks that Sadness is the reason why Riley is sad. In part this is true, but Sadness's main role is to develop an understanding of why others get sad or when Riley herself is sad. You need that understanding to deal with or come to terms with a situation. I can see when people are struggling, when they are masking their emotions. I can see or sense it; I'm not 100% sure how, I just can. However, I struggle to engage and help the person in the right way.

While growing up, I had few friends. I did not understand the reactions of people and remember a number of incidents where I was physically attacked or verbally assaulted. I would like to say that I knew why they happened and the root causes, but in truth, for most of them I do not. One incident I remember very clearly was my friend and I sitting on a bus going home in the early hours of Saturday morning, having a conversation. About ten minutes later, a gentleman who was sitting at the back of the bus got up to get off. As he walked past us he stopped and said to me that if I spoke to him like that he would, in his words, kick the shit out of me. My friend and I just stopped talking and looked at each other. He got off the bus and pointed at me as the doors shut and drove off. To this day, I have no idea what that was about. My friend was also unsure why the man felt the need to speak to me and threaten me. Sadly, this was a situation that I found myself in on more than one occasion and not all of them ended with words.

The main purpose of this project is to expand on my first book (3 Children, 3 Disabilities, 1 Family) which explained how, as a parent, your world seems to stop when you are told that your child has a heart defect which turns out to be a genetic disorder. Later on, you are told your eldest daughter is severely autistic and has ADHD. It shows people how we have dealt with it from the inside.

I wanted to find out how other autistic people dealt with this from their point of view, to find out how it felt when they were first told they were autistic. What did it mean to them? If they could be 'normal', would they want to be?

Imagine, if you can, your daily life is one in which you have your own personal DJ following you, playing at least ten different tracks covering every genre possible. Just for you. Only you can hear it. You arrive at school or work and you are being given instructions. You have to focus on what the person is saying, how they look, how they are reacting, while your own personal DJ is still playing those tracks. Now you have been asked a question. You need to answer it. You open your mouth to answer, but you have forgotten the question. You have not changed your facial expression. You try and process and replay the event to remember the question and open your mouth again to speak. You have processed everything and are ready to reply. Just as your mouth is open and you are about to speak, the person repeats the instruction again but this time they sound or look angry or unhappy. Your DJ has decided to turn the volume up and the response you had has now disappeared. You have forgotten the question again. The person walks off. Your heart is racing. You feel silly that you were unable to answer the question and now the room you are in is getting smaller and smaller. You don't know what to say, how to explain; the words are not coming. Welcome to just one situation that could happen multiple times every day. This one only impacts a few of your senses – imagine your sense of touch was impacted as well. A new fabric conditioner has been used and now your favourite jeans that were so comfy, are now as hard as concrete. You struggle to explain why your jeans feel different and why you are unable to wear them now. You walk into a restaurant, the same one you have been to so many times before, so you are fully aware of what it is like, but they have redecorated. The colours from the walls are screaming at you, jumping off the walls and feel like they are suffocating you. You can't focus and you are clapping and banging your hands on the table. You look up and your mum or dad is there looking at you. Your siblings or best friend have a look of disgust on their faces. (What you believe is a look of disgust anyway.) They are trying to talk to you but all you can hear is their voice through a distorter and they sound like a robot. Not even the latest model from Apple, an iRobot X, just a broken machine from the early 1980s where you can't hear anything, least of all what they are saying.

You have survived going out for dinner. Well done. This may sound extreme, but this is not as uncommon as it seems. The media always seem to show what gets the best reaction from the viewers/readers, the biggest stories in which either this celebrity is having an affair with that celebrity or the disabled child who is unable to speak and hold a spoon. Autism is a spectrum and therefore you will have varying degrees along this spectrum. However, the sensory issues that are detailed above are both in an autistic person who has got a university degree and one who works in the financial services industry. Autism does not define a person; it is something that is part of the person. The same way that having black hair is part of a person born with it. It is part of their DNA. Autism is a condition; I dislike the word disorder as it implies that we are broken and defective which we are not.

Children are brutally honest, and it is only when you start growing up that you start to learn about feelings, your own as well as others. Children learn at different rates; some children do not learn at all. Children on the autistic spectrum find it difficult to understand and struggle to process emotions as well as the reactions of others. Name-calling is something that happens in the school playground everywhere. Children who do not fit in are called 'weird' or 'odd' and sadly, when I was growing up, 'special needs' was slang for being a 'retard' or 'stupid'. The autistic meltdowns and shutdowns that the group explain in detail within these pages, are often seen as extremely childish behaviour, baby behaviour, which may lead to a child getting a nickname. This sticks with the child throughout the rest of their time at that school. The harsh reality of bullying is that it can result in the child being removed and either home schooled or sent to another school. Having to change schools impacts their learning immensely.

As a parent or carer, having an autistic child is hard. It is not for those who do not have serious amounts of inner strength and fight as you will need to be your child's advocate from the first time you get that gut feeling that 'something's not right'. You are not sure what it is but as a parent, you just know. Where do you go for help? Do you go to the school? Your doctor? You discuss your thoughts and feelings with friends and family; some you get support from, others, not so much. Perhaps you are told it is a phase and he or she will 'grow out of it' or 'catch up with the others soon'.

You embark upon endless research, trying to identify each symptom you notice in your child. You try to analyse if this is a behaviour trait or just learning, especially if they are young. You try to explain to the doctor or the school before finally being taken seriously and being referred to a child psychologist who will do an assessment. For us, as parents, we were not sure if our eldest daughter was autistic or had ADD or ADHD. We sat in a room for just over an hour watching the psychologist getting Anabella to explain about her school and talk about her friends. Anabella, at that point, believed very passionately in fairies so much so that she deemed it real. The psychologist said that they were not real. Anabella screamed uncontrollably and came running towards me, crying. It took me a little while to calm her down before taking her back to the psychologist to finish the assessment. She got Anabella to do some colouring and put coloured Lego bricks together. Anabella coloured in a pattern and the bricks were the same pattern. After the tests, the psychologist came and had a quick discussion with me.

She asked what I thought; I explained that my wife thought that our daughter was autistic and I thought she had ADHD. We discussed the reasons as to why we thought that. We had both read a number of articles and books on both of the conditions and some of the common traits as well as some of the common techniques that helped. We tried them. The problem is that the autism and the ADHD fight against each other. Anabella displayed ADHD traits so we put techniques in place. Then the autism came to the forefront so we would try an autism technique and out would come the ADHD. We did not know this at the time, and this is the reason why I think we had different opinions.

The assessment took place on 2nd April 2016 and we were back at the doctors on 5th April to get the results. That moment where the years of struggle and fighting comes to an end. We were going to find out what was different about Anabella, or nothing at all. We sat there while Anabella went off and coloured at the table. The doctor explained that Anabella had moderately severe ASD and ADHD. She had both. It took a while for me to process so I sat there, but thinking about this project, I remember the sad look on the doctor's face. She was delivering bad news and I'm pretty sure she said 'sorry to say' before she delivered it.

I have been hit with that 'sorry to hear that' reaction when I have explained that I have two children with disabilities. Now, after a number of years of promoting disabilities, I refuse to accept it as bad news. I challenge the person who says 'sorry' and explain that the girls are good and there is nothing to be sorry for. I tell them not to assume that they are 'less' of a person because of it. The reaction is normally one of shock upon them being openly challenged. It seems to be an automatic reaction from them to say 'sorry' and now it is an automatic response from me saying 'don't be'. After the reaction of 'sorry', people tend to refer to the stereotypical image that all autistic people are geniuses, like Alan Turing, and can solve complex mathematical problems in seconds or that they are some kind of savant. They think my children must have a photographic memory, perhaps they play the piano flawlessly without even trying, or maybe they are like the nine-year-old autistic child in the film Mercury Rising, who cracked the government code in a puzzle book and they classed him as handicapped.

The harder reactions to deal with actually came from friends and family, who you would think would be the key circle of support. Some of them said that we should get a second opinion; others said that she could not be autistic because she could talk and have a conversation. The stereotypes of autism came out thick and fast after that. You need support as you feel so lost. There are a number of books as well as information on the internet now, but it is not the same. Each child is different. What works for one child, may not work for your child. Friends and family send you everything that they can find online. However, most things do not work as, in my opinion, the most important issue is not said. You need to understand your son or daughter first. You need to work slowly and try and identify what the underlying situations are that cause a reaction. Some may be obvious, and others will not be. Reading a number of guides can be very depressing. I think people read so much that they end up believing everything is in your child when it is not; it is just because you have read it multiple times in the large pile of books which you have now accumulated in the corner. Along with the pile of guides and helpful books, there are large academic books containing years and years of research. The problem with these books is that the volume of material and complex medical references seems to create a gap between the research and theory. It is difficult to equate this with the harsh reality of your child screaming on the supermarket floor because their favourite cereal is not there today, or the company has changed the packaging and therefore it can't possibly be the same cereal.

There are other types of books about autism and other disabilities too. This book falls into the self-help, autobiography type of book; one that explains the struggles and how they have been managed. This book gives hope, but does not give answers to questions such as: why is my three-year-old screaming hysterically and pulling their new white t-shirt off? Why is my son listening to the same song over and over and won't let me change it? Why is my teenage daughter clapping and flapping her hands when we are at the restaurant for a family dinner?

I was introduced to a book called The Reason I Jump. It was written by Naoki Higashida, who was born in 1992 in Japan. He wrote his book at the age of thirteen while still at high school. His autism was severe enough that it impacted his verbal communication. Through a lot of hard work both by Naoki himself as well as his mother and teachers, they managed to use and speak words using an alphabet grid. In England, we would use something such as a qwerty keyboard. I will not spoil the book for you, but this book was the basis for this project. Naoki's thoughts are expressed through his answers to fifty-eight questions commonly asked of autistic people. As well as this, the book contains some proverbs and mini stories which destroy the stereotypical impression that autistic children are social loners who sit in the corner, have no friends and are unable to contribute to anything and society in general.

This could not be further from the truth. Autistic people mostly love company; they just struggle with distractions, understanding and processing the information during these moments. This is especially so if there is a large group or in an area which has lots of distractions, such as a pub. When this happens, they tend to end up in the corner alone or leaving as they are overwhelmed. They do not understand what is going on or perceive that the others do not want them there, so they go. The Reason I Jump was translated from Japanese into English by David Mitchell in 2013. I started reading and could not put it down. It is not a very long book, having fifty-eight questions and some of the answers were very short, but all the questions made me think before I started reading his answers. I had further ideas and questions after the answers, and this was so insightful even to someone who is also autistic, as each one of us is different.

After reading the translated version, I came away from the book loving the concept of questioning an autistic group. I wanted to expand on this idea and have a range of people of varying ages and sexes to answer some deeper questions; questions detailing their home life, childhood, adulthood, work life, relationships as well as the struggles and the best parts of being autistic. My daughter was diagnosed a month before she turned ten and I was diagnosed when I was thirty-five. The diagnoses were for very different reasons; my childhood and school life were very different to my daughter's. The group who volunteered for this project consists of seven people, including myself. The youngest of the group was a thirteen-year-old girl at the time, in secondary school. The oldest is sixty-two. I wanted a group that were still struggling with aspects of their autism and still had questions. A group that had hope in this world and what they would like to see happen as they continue to grow. I wanted the older generations to explain what they went through, what helped them and what didn't, so we do not make the same mistakes, and how society has changed in that time.

As you read these pages, you will get an insight, not only into one autistic person, but a collective group who struggle with things that you may not understand or be able to relate to. You will also see the strength and courage that this group has within themselves and those parents and carers advocating for them. You will see the humour that they have (and I have been lucky enough to enjoy their company while researching and producing this book) and how sociable they are. Reading their words, you will see that they are far from the stereotypical image which is expressed in the media or in the heads of society.

My first book, 3 Children, 3 Disabilities, 1 Family, was published in October 2018 and ended up being a therapy session, not only for me, but also for my wife and our children. It helped us to express what happened during those extremely difficult ten years. We found out what helped, what did not help and what I had learnt over those ten years. I looked at the mistakes I had made (and there have been many) and tried to understand how to not make those again. As a father of three daughters, my youngest enjoyed explaining how she felt as she is not autistic or has any disability and recognises that her elder sisters require more attention. She was brutally honest when she said that she requires attention too and not to forget her – just because she does not need extra help. The hardest thing you will hear as a parent is to be told that you sometimes forget about your child, but it was so important for me to hear that. I set up a specific time for each daughter – just them on their own – so they get all of my attention just for them. As a result, we work better together as a family than before and enjoy our individual time, which I think is equally important.

I want to be clear here that I am not a clinical psychologist, or a doctor or anyone that has studied autism in depth. I am a father who is autistic and knew that I was different to others when I was younger, a few years before I left primary school. At secondary school, it was even clearer to me that I saw things others did not. I struggled with things other found easy. How I saw the world, how I interacted with family and friends. How I spotted things that others did not. I have three daughters. My eldest, Anabella, is diagnosed as having 'moderately severe ASD' as well as having ADHD. My middle daughter, Lucia, has a genetic disorder called 22q11 deletion syndrome, also known as DiGeorge Syndrome, which has traits that run parallel to the autistic spectrum and we have identified certain traits in her which her elder sister and I have. Lucia is a young lady who does not let this disability stop her doing anything she wishes to do. Anabella equally so, and with the support of their parents and their younger sister, Sofia, they have not stopped progressing. I have been raising awareness for all disabilities, especially autism and 22q11 deletion syndrome for nearly ten years.

The Volunteers:

I asked all the volunteers in this project why they decided to be involved and what they would like the readers to come away with after reading it. This is what they collectively hope to bring to you and why they decided to get involved and tell their stories.

Some have chosen to get involved as they struggled when they were younger and want others to be aware of those struggles. Some were bullied, some quite badly, and received no help from either teachers or medical professionals at the time. Some teachers could not help, as they were not informed enough, and others did not want to as the child's problems were deemed to be part of growing up. Some wanted to share their journey of self-discovery. They wanted to learn to understand themselves better; it can be harder for those with a disability to understand themselves when they may not have any role models in the same situation to look up to. Above all, they want to show the world that it is possible to do anything you want, regardless of any disability. It should not stop you chasing and reaching your dreams, and this is an opportunity to show this.

One of the ladies who volunteered to a part of this project is a university graduate. She worked for a global bank and was part of the bank's specific autism internship programme. She struggled to identify with another female on the same level. Research suggests that females 'mask' their autistic, and potentially ADHD, traits better than males and, therefore, it makes it harder to diagnose. The stereotypical assumption of ADHD is that it is explosive and reactionary and therefore obvious to see outwardly. This amazing young lady was neither explosive nor reactionary during my time with her. She explained that she even felt rejected by the autistic community as 'not being autistic enough' and then also rejected by the non-autistic world as 'not fitting in' and 'being weird'. It seems that if you are able to demonstrate a level of self-control over a condition then you are fine. I struggle to understand this level of thinking as it is a very counterproductive statement. This lady went to university and graduated with high honours. She refused to believe that as a female on the autistic spectrum, she should focus on any job she was lucky enough to get, get married and have children as she would not be successful. That is the sort of advice that was given to women back in the 1920s. Be pretty, find a good man and keep a tidy household. That is not the idea we should be selling to our future generations and one that I refuse to sell and promote to my daughters regardless of their disabilities.

These are the main people in the group who helped me and, with the exception of my daughter, Anabella, I have suggested that their real names not be used. Some of the group did not wish to answer certain questions – they were either too difficult to answer, or they decided that they would rather not.

Sally and Michael are both in their early twenties and have both graduated from university. Stephan is a little older also a university graduate.

Anabella is now young lady of fourteen. She was diagnosed just before she turned ten with ADHD and moderately severe ASD. She is the eldest of three daughters and takes medicine for her ADHD. She will be starting her studying for her GCSE's from September 2020.

I am thirty-eight years old; I was diagnosed three years ago in 2017 after a number of incidents at work which required me to get diagnosed to access help. I have worked in the financial services industry for over thirteen years in Human Resources and Reward.

Finally, I have tried to group the questions into the same types of category. The majority of questions either relate to things such as their personal upbringing and experiences or behavioural, theirs as well as others. There are a few general and other questions but mostly link to one or the other. I hope that you enjoy this book, as much as I did researching and speaking with these amazing people over their experiences. I enjoyed writing this book equally as writing my first book for different reasons.

PERSONAL QUESTIONS

Question 1: Did you ever suspect that you were autistic or had any special needs?

There is often a specific incident that makes you seek professional help and confirmation, usually finding something especially challenging compared to your peer group. For example, at university you may question the assignment and struggle to complete it. Tasks seem to be harder for yourself than others. It could be at work, where you end up in a situation in which you may have a 'meltdown'[1].
You may struggle to either understand the situation or explain this to your peer group.

This meltdown is normally the trigger for parents or carers, or themselves if an adult, to research why certain things are difficult or seem to be more difficult for them. This can potentially lead into the long journey to a diagnosis.

Sally realised that she was different to her peer group from the age of nine. She struggled to fit in and to feel accepted, so she acted like the class clown which prompted laughter from her peers and, therefore, she received that feeling of acceptance. She also struggled to have any interest in the same things as her peer group did and couldn't quite understand why they were so fascinated in things such as certain TV shows or activities. A specific incident took place that started the road to diagnosis, which is common. She spoke to a teacher, explaining that she was struggling to understand her peer group. The teacher did not have any answers but helped her understand that people are different and that she saw the world differently. Most importantly, it was OK to not like the same things as others and to have no feelings towards those activities.

Anabella, the youngest member of the group, said that she did not suspect she was autistic as she did not know what it was. She thought of herself as 'crazy'; she explained that she noticed that she acted different to others in her primary school class. The other students in her class and school would say that she was crazy or insane as young children do; therefore, she thought she was. She knew that she always felt different but could never understand why. She was just someone

---

[1] A meltdown is whereby a person with autism temporary loses all control. Triggers build up within the person until they become so overwhelmed that they are unable to talk in any more information and need to be alone.

who always wanted to be the centre of attention and would do anything she could to ensure that happened. Positive or negative attention.

It is especially difficult when you get into trouble at school. The problem with schooling and the education system in general is that it is very stretched to the point of breaking, if not past that point in some areas. All children learn at different rates. Some activities will be harder than others. A child reacts for a number of reasons; it all comes down to level of engagement. If a child is not engaged, then they do not learn or focus, irrespective of a disability. This could be due to frustration if they do not understand the task set by the teacher or even boredom if the task is easy, has been completed and then the child is left alone with no engagement.

Question 2: Do you prefer to be called an 'autistic person' or 'a person with autism'? Does it really matter? and do you care?

This is one that seems to have been getting a lot of noise on social media when this book was thought of, and nearly a year later it is still a thing. Language is important. The use of language is critical to ensure that a person with or without any disability feels engaged and accepted. It will develop the inclusivity that we need.

Everyone wants to be identified as a person first and someone with autism is no different. What autistic people do not want is to be called derogatory names such as retard, weirdo, and other such names. A person who is gay is not a queer or any of the other name calling that takes place. They are a person who happens to like the same sex, that is all. It is important for others to understand the label and give respect.

In terms of an 'autistic person' and 'person with autism', neither seem to have generated much care from those in this book. Michael has a personal preference to be called a person with autism as well as reinforcing that everyone is a person first. Others, like Stephan, Roger, Sally and myself could not care less and seem to think that this difference is a society issue, overthinking what a person should be called when actually, a person is a person with a name and should be treated as such, regardless of race, gender, sexual orientation, or any disability. That is a world which everyone wants. It seems that society, especially the media (mainstream and social), seem to want to give their opinions, regardless of if they are asked or not. Even some medical professionals say that you should call them a 'person with autism'. Personally, I prefer to be called Dave when I am speaking to someone and I will call myself 'autistic' if I want. For those of you who wish to give your opinion – don't – just ask. Ask the person themselves rather than assume that you know what is best for me or anyone else.

The best response to this came from Anabella (who is at secondary school), who said that she does not care which of the two people call her. She said the world will see her and her condition how they wish to see it anyway, regardless of which label the media attach to it this week. She is a human being, a young girl growing up, who just happens to have a disability (actually two). She is right. The world does seem to see what it wishes to see and hopefully these pages will help the world see things differently.

Question 3: Have you always been autistic? You don't look autistic.

Yes, funnily enough autism is not something that you either develop or grow out of. It is something that you are born with; it is part of your DNA and not caused by too much 'screen time'. You may read this and feel that it is a strange question, but this is asked more times than you realise. This, and being told that the person doesn't believe that an autistic person is actually autistic. I personally have been asked this more than twenty times in the last two years and at least five of those who asked, refused to believe I was autistic, based on my work role and how I interact with others. The rest of the group have all confirmed that they have been asked if they are actually autistic and also not believed by at least one person. Being challenged and told that I am not autistic and shouldn't say that I am, is quite soul-destroying in a way. It is also very insulting. Imagine, if you can, that you explain to someone that you are gay and they respond by saying, of course you are not gay as you play rugby. Well, Gareth Thomas captained Wales playing rugby union for a long time before he publicly spoke out as being gay. Those same people would not insult him by telling him that he is not gay.

The group, quite rightly, find this question a little bit hard to deal with. Some reacted with eye rolls, some became withdrawn and others got angry and frustrated. They felt that a person would have to be quite ignorant to even ask that. This is mainly because when that question is asked, it is asked in a 'I don't believe you' type of voice and attitude. Anabella and Michael have explained that sometimes they have responded with an equally odd question which is met with a range of reactions. They have asked things such as 'have your eyes always been that colour?' Other responses from the group include the following: 'I am wearing my jeans today, instead of my special autistic trousers', or 'you don't look ignorant but …'

Autism is something that, at the moment, is believed to be something you are born with. The genes or markers of autism are there in the DNA and are a part of that person in the same way that your DNA markers mean that you have blue eyes. You cannot get rid of it like a cold with Ibuprofen. However, some of the group believe that potentially, some of their autistic traits are influenced by their environment and the support system in place. So, how an autistic child without support grows up will be different to an autistic child with support. The belief is that the more supported child will be less expressive and more able to control, mask, or develop techniques which will allow them to identify or reduce any traits which later become very expressive. This does not mean that the autism 'disappears'.

Sally and Michael explained that they got support when they were younger. As a result, they expressed a greater depth of understanding about themselves and some of the social issues that they have faced. They both spoke about having little to no social skills. With the support they received, they were able to develop those skills along with their peers. Their peers were aware of the issues that they both faced and were supportive.

Those who did not have that support network, like me, were often found to be dismissed by peers and adults alike. This happened throughout our schooling and early years of work. We were all unable to develop friendships at school and unable to understand and learn about our peers and relationships in general – from family, friendships to even romantic relationships – and why we could not have friends like others did. We were also not taught any techniques to help us and had to learn and develop those skills by ourselves in later life.

Sally has explained that she felt she was dismissed from both the autistic community and the non-autistic community. When explaining why she felt like this, she said it was because she was able to mask her behaviour traits really well. On the inside she was racing and concentrating so hard that she was mentally drained, but on the outside, however, she was calm and gave the impression she was like everyone else. She was given lots of support when she was younger and was therefore able to learn how to manage her typical autistic behaviour. Therefore, autistics do not believe that she is really autistic. The problem with non-autistic people, is that most instantly think of the worst-case typical traits of a person clapping or jumping uncontrollably in the corner. The same way that anyone who has seen Harry Potter will automatically think of Daniel Radcliffe playing him as this is who you have been told is Harry Potter. The media portrays all autistics as someone who is obsessed with order; someone who colour-codes things, regardless of what it is; someone who is a maths genius. Therefore, she is shunned by the non-autistic's as someone who cannot possibly be autistic as she does not fall into that image they have seen. In short, she is damned on both sides.

Some of the group brush off these comments and move on. They try not to let it bother them. They admit that some days are better than others. The more that their autistic condition is ignored or even challenged as false, the harder those days are. Others are up front about being autistic and therefore are not challenged or asked as much now as they are in their late thirties and forties. However, they still get overwhelmed in certain situations and new people to the team who are not aware, tend to think that the person is not professional in their behaviour.

I have had a complaint about me at work when I had a mini meltdown during a conference call. I was unable to get my point across and the sensory environment that I was in was not conducive to my ability to stay calm. As a result, my autism was challenged and for a time not believed.

The younger members of the group try and ignore it as best as possible. They used to explain that just because they could walk in a straight line or have a conversation without shouting out or making noises, it did not mean that they were not autistic. Autism is a scale; they are on one end of the scale compared to others at the other end. They cannot help the thought process or the idea of what someone thinks an autistic person should be. They will be them and if people don't want to believe them, then don't. Just leave them alone and cease commenting.

Question 4: Do you ever wonder what it would be like to not be autistic, to be 'normal'?

'Yes' was the instant response from Anabella and Sally as well as others. I admit that I have often thought about this in my younger days as well (before I was diagnosed but knowing I was different to others). They said they have always wondered what it would be like to be normal. Then they both stopped talking and looked around the room. They started to think about what that would mean. They were not sure what they would be giving up. Sally asked for her autism to be like a light switch. She could then switch it off when it gets too much – when her anxiety becomes too much; when she gets too much stimulus and overloads. Michael explained he liked that idea and would use it for large group situations which he always finds the hardest to overcome. These overloads can happen in various situations, such as a crowded tube travelling home.

Slowly, during the conversation discussing the good and bad points of autism, the whole group realised that being autistic is great. When asked again if they wanted to be 'normal', the answer was 'no' almost immediately from everyone. Although all of us still wonder what it would be like to not have autism, to be able to not have meltdowns or sensory overload and to enjoy situations more than we do sometimes. It can really take its toll on a person and is very difficult to explain here with words on paper. However, they would not want to give up autism. They love their brain; they love how it works (most of the time) and how it sees the world.

They would like some of the social difficulties removed, like anyone else who would like to be better at something. Others question, what is normal? If normal is to be exactly the same as everyone else, then they do not want to be 'normal'. They love this part of themselves and they feel that they have a good quality of life, even if work and university was, and still is very difficult. This is the area that they would like to change but not to be a clone of someone. I do not think anybody wants to be like everyone else. Everyone wants to be themself.

Anabella loves being autistic, and she cannot imagine being anything else. She expressed normal as a mock insult. She does not want to be like everyone else. She wants to be her. What does society deem as normal, she asked? I was speechless. What could I reply to that? I was not sure then, and am even less sure now, how to answer that question. She says that the media seems to change the definition of normal every day; a woman should look like this one week and then like something else the next. A man should be a hard-muscular man, like the old Diet Coke adverts, then he should be in touch with his feelings and cry the next. He should have a visible six-pack at all times and if not, then he is not healthy or looking after his body. The media loses its mind once in a while when it says you should be both and then quickly dismisses it the next day. For someone so young and still finding out about herself, she seems to have a better understanding and handle of society's views than I do.

Question 5: How did you feel when you were told you were autistic?

Relief. Acceptance. Understanding. All words used by the group to explain the feeling when they were told. Some were diagnosed young, around six or seven. Others in their teens or the late stages of secondary school. Others were not diagnosed until their mid-thirties, like me. Sally, Anabella, and Michael have all got ADHD as well as autism. Michael was diagnosed first with ADHD when he was six. He was relieved as it helped with the acceptance of the manic behaviour, the hyper playground energy that he was displaying. Later, when he was diagnosed with autism as well, it was a different feeling of relief. This enabled his parents to fight for support to help him at school. He explained that his parents were relieved and understood; they now knew that with the right support and environment, he would be able to fulfil his potential.

Sally was the opposite in that her parents did not tell her. She found out by accident. She was searching in her parents' room for paper and found the letter. The letter went into detail explaining that, at first, they suspected she had a split personality disorder before confirming an autism diagnosis instead. Relief and acceptance were not the feelings she had at that point. Instead, it was confusion and anger. She flipped out and had a major argument with her parents over it. To some degree, she thinks that her parents refused to believe that she was autistic at first. When her routine was disrupted and broke down, she would not have a typical meltdown but a funny moment in which she would shout out "I'm going autism!". This was her way of expressing that she was unable to process the change, that her routine had changed.

A good story retold by Sally was about a Christmas event. She was told to get ready for dinner; no specific information was given to her at that point – she was just told to get ready for dinner. She disappeared and got dressed in some simple jeans and a jumper. When she came downstairs, the rest of the family were all dressed up. Unfortunately, this resulted in a flip out. There was lots of crying by Sally and a fundamental lack of understanding as to why everyone was dressed up as she hadn't been told this. End result, she didn't go. She later felt really guilty. This event was then discussed and they worked out how all parties could handle it better next time.

After a diagnosis, more time and effort are spent trying to understand these 'meltdowns' or what changes impact them, such as sensory overload. This is essential for two reasons: 1) The autistic person needs to understand what could impact/affect them so they know for potential future events, and 2) others need to know what could trigger a reaction so they can plan things better and avoid situations which could cause sensory overload.

Anabella did not think about it at the time; she was nine. She did not know what autism was and thought that this was something that most people had. After a while she asked me to explain what autism was. I tried to explain which helped her have a better understanding. She could see some of the traits we discussed and how they impacted her. She explained that she mostly felt confused and struggled to understand her reactions to things. She said it was very hard to prepare for something if she didn't know why she reacted in a certain way last time. She spends a lot of time trying to work out if her reaction is a result of her autism, ADHD, simply her growing up, or a brand-new situation which she needs to learn about. She still has moments now and likes to think of herself as a little girl growing up like everyone else, just with a few quirks. She spends a lot of time wondering if she is quirky due to her autism or whether she would be quirky irrespective of that.

I was diagnosed recently as autistic. I showed no emotions when I was 'formally' told as I had suspected this for a number of years, always knowing that I saw the world differently. I do not think I felt relief. For me, it was good to know that this was finally confirmed as I was struggling with my work life at that time and the interactions were causing mental health issues. Thinking about this as I am writing now, maybe the feeling was relief as I now knew that I could get some support when I needed it. Sadly, I was not given support, even after the diagnosis, and ended up leaving as a result. Maybe it was more acceptance that I felt, as just like my daughter, I have always been quirky and now those quirky traits could be recognised and given a name.

Question 6: Do you tell people that you are autistic?

The group was split over this question. Some are very open and explain it to new people straight away. Others will discuss it if the conversation naturally brings it up. Others will not say it at all or will not tell certain people. For example, people that they are dating. Others have chosen not to tell their workplace as they have previously had negative issues which they believe were a result of being autistic and being open about it.

All the group have acknowledged that when they have explained that they are autistic, they are not believed from the outset. Comments such as 'are you sure?', 'you must have it very mildly then' or the groups' favourite, 'you don't look autistic'. The autistic community, as well as each member of this group, would like to know what an autistic person looks like, mainly because we don't know.

Not all autistic people are non-verbal and sit and clap or rock. There are people at that end of the spectrum but each autistic person is different. Each member of the group seems to have a circle of friends who know that they are autistic and are their safe group. These are the friends who can be told that they have had enough of people and they won't react negatively against them. That acceptance is there, for the majority of the time. These groups understand and have awareness that their autistic friend could react differently to them in different situations.

Anabella used to tell people that she was autistic after diagnosis, but she was met with negative comments or the bullying that she encountered got worse – now she has decided that she will only tell some people and only after she has built up a level of trust with them beforehand. She explains that this trust needs to be built up slowly and it is done for two reasons. Firstly, because most people do not believe she is autistic. They think that she is seeking attention. She has been called the 'so-called autistic girl' and bullying takes place worse than before. Secondly, to protect herself. She had difficulties at her primary school which have continued into secondary school, caused by her clearly being different to her peer group, and sadly she feels that she is an easy target.

Question 7: Do you have any family members that are also autistic?

The majority of the group seem to have someone in their family that is also autistic. Younger siblings or parents being most common. There are a few studies and reports that seem to suggest that autism could be heredity. Others in the group believe that some family members have a lot of the traits of the autistic spectrum but they have not been formally diagnosed.

Anabella explained that even though her dad, me, is also autistic it did not make it easier for her. Others, like Michael, explained that it had no impact on him because he was the elder sibling and first diagnosed. Anabella and I seem to have a love-hate relationship and clash constantly as both of us are very literal. We both struggle with change and have our own ways of dealing with things, which are sometimes the opposite of each other. This can, therefore, cause more anxiety and clashes. However, we both agree that when one of us has a meltdown, the other one is the best person to help them through it.

Anabella explained her relationship with her mum; she compares it to a Jekyll and Hyde type of relationship. They are either the very best of friends where nothing can get between them, or they are the worst of enemies, in which case – look out. It tends to depend on the situation. Anabella explains that in some ways it is very helpful that her dad is autistic; he can explain things in a way that she can relate to, most of the time. But the best part is having her mum there. She says that her mum is the person who can see what the young girl is thinking or feeling. Her mum has learnt a number of different things that help to calm her down, such as sitting on the sofa and giving her a cuddle to telling her to play the piano or draw a picture. Providing her with craft activities seems to be the best way to help her at home.

Question 8: What does autism mean to you?

Anabella responded by explaining that she doesn't know what it means to her. She understands that autism as well as her ADHD is something that she was born with, like others have blonde hair. It is a part of her, and her body and she cannot do anything about it. She sat proudly and smiled while finishing with the best simple response so far. "It is me, in full."

The older members of the group said it was everything. It is part of their personality. Autism is the reason why they see the world as they do, why they feel the world the way they do. How they interpret things differently to others. Autism is them.

I completely agree with the group on this. I am proudly autistic. I see it as part of me and my personality. I would not be me without my autism. I know I struggle with some things and I react very differently to others in certain situations (not always in a positive way); I cannot always control that. But this is the whole me. What you see is what you get. For those of you that know me, you never worry about whether I really mean what I say or question my integrity. I will be direct with everyone I meet, maybe too direct.

Question 9: Do you have any other condition aside from autism?

Three members of the group also have ADHD along with their autism. Each one is different. ADHD is an explosive instant, a short burst and then over. Autism is a longer, slower event that builds up or dissipates over time. Michael and Sally oppose each other as to which is easier to control. Michael believes that his ADHD is easier to control and uses medicine to do this. He is more aware of his ADHD traits and therefore he can manage to control them better when recognised. Michael also feels that after an ADHD burst that he is able to reflect upon the reason behind it in order to manage it better next time round.

Sally, on the other hand, finds that her autism is easier to control. She finds that as autism is longer and has more of an impact on her day-to-day life, that she has been able to manage it better. She has had more experience and is really good at masking her autistic behaviour and traits. The issue she finds with managing her autism is that it is mentally extremely draining as she has to concentrate which uses up a lot of energy all day.

Anabella is not sure which one is harder. She is still learning about her body as well as herself growing up. The joys of being a teenager. She is unsure which traits are due to her autism or her ADHD. She is learning how to control and manage each trait. She has medicine for the ADHD and therefore she is making an assumption that this is harder to control as there is no medicine for her autism. However, she is not sure and says that when she works it out, she will let me know.

Question 10: *Autistic people take things literally, have you ever mistaken your belief or imagination for reality?*

The group, on the whole, understand the difference between reality and imagination. However, Anabella expressed that when she was at primary school, she struggled to understand the difference when it came to some realistic situations. The example she gave was with regard to Hogwarts School in Harry Potter. She was ten and she knew that she would be leaving her primary school and going to secondary school soon. For her birthday in May (just after you are told which secondary school your child will be attending), she was given a Harry Potter package. Inside was a wand, games, and all sorts of stationary to do with Harry Potter. There was also a letter which said that she had been accepted into Hogwarts School in September.

As going to a new school in September was a real event and having received the Hogwarts' letter, she believed that she was actually going to go to Hogwarts. She did not understand when her parents explained that she would be going to the local high school instead. She would produce the letter and show it to her parents. She understands the difference now, but she admits that she still struggles if the imagination or belief is closely aligned to something in real life.

Sally explained that she has very vivid dreams. They feel so real when she wakes up that she believes it was real. After waking up properly and considering things in the morning, she understands that it was a dream and not real, but it takes a while to process this. When she was younger, she would explain these dreams to her parents as though they were real. Growing up seemed to help that distinction between imagination and reality.

Question 11: If there was a cure for autism, would you take it?

Yes… Probably … Hang on, not sure … Maybe, actually no … Definitely not.

If autism could be a light switch which you can turn on and off, then yes. When things get too much then you could switch it off and not let your anxiety increase to a level which could result in a meltdown.

Michael has a fierce pride of being autistic. He and others within the group wear it like a badge over their heart. They believe that it is a part of their personality, their character, their person. It is the funny side of themselves; the ability to look at things differently; the way they form pictures in their mind. If they could keep all this and more, they would be more tempted.

All of us recognise that having autism is not easy or fun. In fact, sometimes we understand that it is pretty rubbish, to be honest. We remain upbeat and focus on the good bits, of which there are many. Sally explains that although she complains, makes numerous mistakes, and was bullied because she was different, she is scared that if a cure took her autism away, she would be a different person. She would become 'normal'. Anabella said that her experiences with 'normal' people have not been very positive so far, so she does not want to be one of them.

The group also commented that they believe that most autistic people would not want a cure either. It feels like it would be taking something away from them. However hard it is sometimes and however much they struggle from one day to the next, they would not want someone to take something away from them.

During the group's discussions around a cure for autism, all of them agreed that there are a lot of benefits to being autistic in terms of thinking differently to others. How they see problems and how they find solutions. Most have a very singular logical way to approaching and resolving issues. How they process information very differently and how information is articulated. Socially, they are very different to their peers, and all agree that this is the biggest challenge, combined with the ignorance around autism. Older members, such as I, have learnt to deal with situations which were previously difficult.

Others, like Sally and Michael, have learnt how not to deal with things by not putting themselves in that situation, or by removing themselves as soon as possible.

There are five words which all members said sum up this group. I wouldn't go as far as assuming this would be the case for the rest of the autistic community, but I think the majority would agree that 'I don't know any different'.

Question 12: What feelings do you experience when you are having during one of your extreme highs?

Sally and I both agree that during our extreme highs all of our senses seem to be heightened. We are more alert, more aware of our surroundings. We seem to notice more things. Sally says that she is very good in terms of responses or in her ability to process information during these situations. This is the very best of her. Like Spiderman or any other superhero. She can also be a little irrational and silly as she has so much energy; too much energy for her to use in such a short period of time.

These extreme highs that are experienced by Sally do not last long, as they are so mentally draining. She believes they last a maximum of ten minutes; on average they last five to six minutes. Normally, she is very relaxed and calm, so it is noticeable to everyone else around when this happens.

Others find this a problem because there are too many feelings, thoughts and emotions running through their brain to process. They tend to take themselves away and just go through everything slowly, in a safe environment. Michael said that he can come up with some of the best ideas, personally and workwise, during these moments, but he does recognise that he is generally too much for other people to handle during this time.

I describe it as being the Energiser Bunny on Red Bull and speed. It lasts for no more than ninety seconds, but a very fast paced, explosive ninety seconds. Most of us feel that these extreme high moments seem to be event driven.

Question 13: Can you describe an extreme low?

Extreme lows are different for each person. Sally explained that she has two types of 'down' moments. One is called a 'shutdown' and the other is a 'meltdown'. Her version of a meltdown is different to what others class as a meltdown.

A 'shutdown' is something that happens once a week on average for her. It is when her body and brain need a way to wind down. Shutdowns can be a few hours, or a whole day, in which she will lay still with music in the background and have no interaction with anyone. During the working week, she is concentrating so hard on her behaviour and managing her autistic traits that she is physically and mentally exhausted, and her body and brain requires this shutdown at the end of the week. Like a laptop crashing and needing to be reset. Every IT department tells you to reboot the system; this is the human equivalent. These shutdowns prevent the more drastic meltdown occurring.

A 'meltdown', for Sally, is something that happens maybe once or twice a year. This is when she is unable to function at all. She will be completely unresponsive and will sit in a room and rock, waving and clapping her hands at anything and everything. This could also last for a few hours through to a whole day in extreme cases.

The triggers for these two very different extreme lows that occur is the compound effect of everything that is going on. It is not normally a specific trigger that causes either low point.

There are physical symptoms which allow Sally and others to recognise that a shutdown or meltdown may be imminent. Her body changes, she becomes snappier, and struggles to focus on any topic or event. She is less engaged socially, and her normal calm relaxed manner seems to be absent.

When having an extreme low, most of the group feel that they do not want to engage with anyone and want to be left alone or walk away, regardless of who they are with or where they are. It could be family, partner or even a close friend. A lot of the group confirmed that a number of relationships have broken down because of this. They take themselves away and therefore the other person believes that the issue is because of them. It is not.

The biggest difficulty, which I believe is how relationships break down, is that autistic people cannot explain and articulate this feeling at the time. They are unable to process, speak and explain to the people that mean a lot to them, what is going on. What they need at this time is to be left alone for a while. They will manage this themselves as they have always done and when they are engaged again, it can be discussed.

Question 14: What would you want to tell someone new who would like to get to know you?

The group, in general, would love to tell new people some of the issues they struggle with, so they can be prepared: situations such as shutdown moments or the inability to articulate why they do not want to do something socially, even if it is arranged in advance. However, the reality is very different.

Most seem to explain and discuss the fact that they are autistic, but only if it comes up in conversation. They will only express certain things and never in great detail. Most are still very guarded from previous experiences, myself included. It is difficult for them to explain what autism is and how it impacts them as this is the norm for them. It is difficult for a non-autistic person to understand as they will never experience it.

It is like someone explaining that they have blue eyes and the other person has brown. There is no reason behind it; you were born with that eye colour. There is nothing to explain as to the why or how.

The group do not like being put into what society seems to see as the 'autism box', i.e. all autistic people should look like this and act like that. That is not the case; it is not even close. They are as individual and unique as everyone else and that is what makes them, and everyone else, amazing. Accept them for who they are. Faults, struggles and all, and if you cannot do that, leave them in peace. They have enough to deal with without others adding to it.

Others feel that some people, when they find out, seem to look for something specific. They try to understand every behaviour and analyse it. Some may even have a background in psychology or some brief understanding of autism. Michael remembered that during an event he attended, he met someone with a master's degree in behaviour psychology. This person tried to explain how best an autistic person learns and put all autistic people in the same box, including him. Each person learns in a different way, regardless of autism or any other disability.

Do not try and analyse this group or others, get to know the person first and then you can discuss autism or some of their traits as and when they appear.

Question 15: Did you enjoy your primary and secondary school?

Not really. Without the support and help that they desperately needed, they were bullied, had no friends, and were shunned. This is not an exaggeration. They were deemed as the weird outcasts and an easy target for anyone, sometimes teachers as well as students. Some of the group expressed that they were so depressed that they considered suicide. Two members of the group sadly even attempted this. Some did not have the support of parents, other family members, or even the school. Others had this support but these people were limited as to what help they could provide.

My experience of both primary and secondary school was terrible. I had no idea and was outcasted during primary, but it did not impact me as much as secondary school did. Secondary school was worse. I was bullied a lot. I lost my idea of things, including relationships and friendships. I was getting into trouble with teachers and for the majority of it I did not understand why and what I had done wrong. I got no support inside or outside of school. I was not diagnosed and was labelled as a troublemaker. I had to work out everything for myself. I managed to do it eventually, but it is still impacting me now nearly twenty-five years later.

Some of the group moved schools constantly. They never got to enjoy it and therefore look back at the school years as something very negative with a lack of support. Others moved schools and that one school was the turning point for them in a positive way.

Sally and Michael went to a boarding school. Sally moved there at the age of fourteen and she loved it from that moment on. Prior to this move, she hated school and was constantly moving around. The difference was the support she received; the acceptance, but discipline, that the boarding school gave her. They accepted her condition but did not allow her to use her autism or ADHD as an excuse to misbehave. She made friends and was able to have her alone time.

Sally and Anabella recognised individual teachers in their school who tried their best to help them. They may not have enjoyed school, but this teacher or member of staff helped them in different ways. One helped Sally to understand how to interact socially and develop techniques to reduce the sudden outbursts that she had. She developed those skills further with friends and used those techniques to keep them in a safe space. Anabella remembers one teacher that supported her with extra things she needed in class, so she could be independent and do the work that was set.

Primary school seems to be the worst period for the majority of the group. They all explain that they were bullied in varying degrees either by students or sometimes by teachers who would try different methods to attempt to make the child be like everyone else. An outburst from an autistic child was mainly seen as severely disruptive behaviour. The reality is that any disruptive behaviour is generally a reaction to something, I do not disagree that the behaviour is disrupting the other children in class and it needs to be managed, but children are not disruptive for the sake of it. It is a reaction to something and part of learning is to identify the reason and help the child next time.

Some of the group have ADHD as well as autism. They had more energy than their peer group and certain activities were extremely easy for them. When they had finished the work, they were expected to sit still in class. This could be for over twenty minutes while waiting for others to finish. Children find it very difficult to sit still for over twenty minutes, without a book, phone, or TV. My children have certainly never managed to do this. It would not work for any child; they get bored and play up. Why would an autistic child be any different?

Sally and Michael explained that for English and reading they were above average for their age group and therefore they both got easily bored with the work set. This created frustration for both them and the teachers alike. Teachers were unable to deal with them as they had other children to teach. However, both Sally and Michael were extremely poor in maths. They were below expectations for their age group. This created a different level of frustration for both them and the teachers. This time, the disruptive behaviour was because they did not understand and got frustrated, instead of boredom. Michael played up when he was frustrated and this resulted in him being removed so he did not have to do maths. He soon learnt to play up on purpose every maths lesson to get out of it, so he no longer felt frustrated. However, the underlying issue and teaching were never addressed.

I was the opposite to Sally and Michael. I was extremely good at maths. In secondary school, my maths teacher knew this. At the beginning of the lesson, he would give me additional work. Then, when I did finish and he was busy with other students, I had something to do so that I did not cause a disruption. I struggled with English. However, during my working career, working for large financial banks, this has improved. I think the reason why I excelled at maths and was below par for English is because maths is absolute. $1+1=2$. It always will. However, English is ambiguous, and some words have double meanings depending on how they are used. This is where I struggled to process.

Secondary school was amazing for the majority of the group. Despite the first few years being difficult, there was support from certain teachers or heads of departments who knew how best to deal with them. Also, as they grew up and started to understand themselves more, they also liked themselves more. They became engaged with teachers; the work and subjects in which they flourished were pushed further, and extra help was given to the basics and foundations that they did not have from primary school.

They found ways to work together. The world is like that; you have to work together. A teacher cannot teach if the child is not engaged at all. A child cannot learn, no matter how excited they are about the subject, if a teacher is not engaging with them.

Question 16: How did you find University?

Those who went to university loved it. The first year seemed to be the hardest, especially the first term. But the second term was very different to the first term. Some were more comfortable coming from a boarding school environment to university but equally they had other challenges.

At university they had a large group of friends, they were accepted and were not put into a set 'box' like they were in primary and secondary school. Schools are focusing on one route. At university, you are a young adult and are responsible for yourself, not being dependent on your lecturers or parents/guardians.

Those who went to university were already diagnosed and supported from day one. Some were given a mentor who helped them. The mentor ensured that they remained on track with their studies and gave them an opportunity to discuss any issues with the course, university, or a subject lecturer. It was an opportunity to discuss other things too, such as about themselves as a person. One of the group lost a family member who they were extremely close to and therefore ended up getting very emotional. The situation was extremely difficult for them to process. It took a number of days to do this and they were therefore given extra help during this time.

Michael found university a place where he could put all those foundation life skills he learnt into practice. Real independence: how to deal with conflict, managing money and general day-to-day life. He had to deal with issues which created a level of anxiety. Sometimes he had to not deal with issues and learn how to pick which battles to engage in and which to walk away from. For example, having to discuss with roommates the tidiness of the apartment. He had to learn how to engage and explain when he got into that extremely low moment. Mainly, he had to learn about himself and friendships and the different type of friendships that you could have with people.

Others still had to battle for things, but this time they had to be their own advocate instead of their parents or other family members doing so on their behalf. This gave them a new understanding and perspective of what their parents or friends had gone through all those years. They also learnt that there seemed to be a clear discrimination between a physical disability and an invisible one, such as autism. Some of the most obvious discrimination that they received was given by people with a physical disability.

The university had advocates to act on his behalf, but when Michael explained that he needed certain things to enable him to progress through his degree, he was dismissed by a person in a wheelchair saying that he did not need that level of support and that there were others, like themselves, who need more. This was very hard to understand and process, let alone made even more difficult when the Student Support Services were not acting well for him. This creates a physical barrier making an already hard job, harder.

On a positive, the battles that the group members have had to fight have made them realise one very important lesson; a lesson which is key and the biggest life lesson there is. It is that, as individuals, they have the power. They are the only ones that can fight for what they need; they have to push for it. They realised and appreciated much more than ever what their parents did for them when they were younger, especially when they were having issues at primary and secondary school and were tirelessly fighting for the support. They never understood when they were younger that when they and their school friend had a problem, why the friend got help and they did not seem to.

Autism is not something that is going to stop when you hit twenty-five. Yes, you can learn to manage some of the traits and situations, but only up to a point. Some of the group were part of the autistic intern scheme at a large financial services company. They described the scheme as amazing and so empowering that were able to raise any issues that happened unlike at schools and university.

Question 17: Not many autistic people go to University or find it too overwhelming, what would you say to any considering it?

Just do it. You will only learn when you are outside your comfort zone and by pushing yourself. Life is full of change and you will need to develop those skills to adapt. You will not be protected as much as when you were a child; as an adult you need to be able to look after yourself. Sally explained that it is extremely important for everyone, especially autistic people, to build their resilience and confidence and to manage change as much as possible.

You get to pick what you want to do. You are not forced to learn what they want to teach, like in primary and secondary school. You are an individual and this is the doorway to adulthood. You will get the support if you are open minded. Sally explains that the difference between school, university and working life is this: school is structured and university is half structured. Uni wants you to be the person you want to be. In your working life, you are all on your own and expected to work. Depending on what work you do, you are reacting more to situations. During work, you are expected to use problem-solving skills and resolve any issues you come across. There is help and you can and should ask for it if unsure, but the responsibility of the work is yours and yours alone.

There are more social aspects in university, like societies to join to meet other like-minded individuals. You learn new skills and make new friendship groups, increasing your self-worth and employment potential. It is a structured route into employment; there is employment support such as workshops to practice interviews. It may not be advertised or well known, but there will be other autistic people there.

Sally says that it is critical that you are 100% open with the university over your autism, or you could be battling with them from day one. There is a variety of support available. For example, you could get slides in advance so you are engaged in the lesson. Michael had a note taker which he found was key so he could focus on the learning aspect as opposed to making his own notes, as both of those skills were difficult for him.

Ask yourself, why do you think that you cannot go to university? It is an assumption that you cannot do it, rather than a fact. You need to break the reasons down and work out what aspects of university life you think you will struggle with. You can then discuss them with the university to ensure that the support is in place for when you begin. I do not regret many things in my life, even all the difficulties that I have gone through and there are many, but one regret I have is not going to university. It would have been extremely hard for me. I have no doubt about that, but I trust in my own ability more now than I did then.

Go and visit a university and speak to other autistic people who are there or have recently graduated and check out the support services available to you. There will be support for you; however, you will have to work hard for it. It is very different to school and is a learning curve. You must realise that when you get to university, you are an adult. You are expected to independently take this on. It is your degree and any help and support that you need is your responsibility to obtain.

Sally asked what was the worst that could happen? You get there and not like it. Before you make a rash decision, stick with it for a while, explain your feelings and thoughts to the support services. Explain to your friends, family and get other advice. If you still feel that university is not for you, then leave. University is not the making and breaking of you as a person.

Question 18: Do you have flashback memories?

Memory seems to be different for each member of the group. Sally feels her memory is bizarre and there is not much sense to it. She does not have flashback memories like you see in the movie scenes and she is not sure exactly how her memory works. One thing that is key for her memory flashback is smell.

She lived and travelled around Thailand for a period of time. While she was out there, she walked into a place where the cleaning fluid was really strong and instantly a flashback memory took place. In her mind, she went back to her school where they used similar cleaning products, and she could picture the school hallway clearly: the white walls, with black marks from bags; the cheap chequered flooring in the canteen; the cook in the kitchen shouting about food; and the dinner lady that used to cut her apples for her. She used to cut the skin off of her apples in a spiral motion and Sally would have a pile of apple peelings which she would eat at lunchtime.

Sound is the other most common memory trigger amongst the group. A piece of music can take the person back to a certain event and they will relive the same emotions and feelings that happened during that song or even what situation that song represents. My daughter and I both have music playing all the time; it helps us focus and we both relive situations when certain songs are played.

Question 19: What is the worst thing about being autistic?

It is so draining. It is so hard to concentrate for so long and so intensely. It is exhausting trying to mask the different feelings, emotions and 'quirks' all the time. It feels like you have to always be on your guard. Sally described it as being on pure adrenaline all the time.

Michael says the worst thing is the lack of understanding and sometimes the ignorance of others about his condition. Many people have the idea that all autistic people are the same, or because they may know one autistic person, that they think that they know you or what you need to do to be better. Anabella said that the worst part is explaining to her friends, and even some of her extended family, that this is not something she is going to grow out of. She says that there seems to be an idea, especially initially, that when she grows up, she will be fine and her autism will not be an issue anymore.

I feel that this is not the worst part for me, but one of the biggest challenges is the changes that take place over time. When I was younger, it was hard and stressful following the social rules that I was taught either by parents, friends, or the educational system. As a child I was given a bigger allowance when I messed up. Sometimes I was given additional help. The situation would have been explained to me again, or I was given more time to understand and process the situation. Those social rules are enforced and re-enforced when required during childhood.

As an older adult, the feelings could be just as, or even more so, overwhelming as they were when I was younger. But now, the allowance given to you is much smaller. Sometimes there is not any allowance at all. It is not socially acceptable as an adult to have a meltdown or outburst as you did when you were at school. You are now judged on society's expectations which are a lot higher.

What is acceptable and reasonable for others are not the same for this group, but this group want to be part of society and interact with everyone. We just need a little more time to process than you might find acceptable.

Question 20: Do you think you would like to be 'normal'?

'Always think about it' said the majority of the group. They like the idea of a cure and they smile at the thought of it. While discussing being normal, they realise all the things that makes them unique. Autism is a part of them, and they cannot push it out: the humour that they have; the fight and belief within themselves to not be defined by media stereotypes, by ignorant people saying they will never achieve anything. That is a result of being autistic.
The only way this group would consider being 'normal' is if what they would lose could be quantified. If the personality traits that mean the most to them were on that list, then the answer would be shouted from the rooftops. That answer would be a resounding no, not a chance.

Anabella and I are immensely proud of being different and challenge the idea of what 'normal' is. We understand that every person, regardless of a disability or not, has quirks. They see things differently to others as well as differently to an autistic person. Why would we and other members of this group want to swap our logical approach to things? The group have a clear definition of approach and noise. Emotions seem to be put in the 'noise' section when trying to process anything.

One of my working roles is as a senior project manager within large corporate companies. Over the course of my career, I have managed large teams, some over thirty people, and have dealt with numerous projects which have short deadlines or projects which feel that you are constantly up against it. During these high stress times, others around me seem to be very emotional over the deadline, questioning things such as how people will react to the project. How will this deadline be achieved? How do I explain that this approach will not work for someone else? While everyone is feeling the pressure, I seem to be relatively calm, majority of the time. The approach to the problem is still the same, my logic is tested and retested and I adapt, if required, but the emotional part is noise to me. It makes no difference to the outcome whether I am calm or anxious. In fact, I would say emotions would have a negative impact. I trust in my ability and I have belief that my logical approach is correct. I tell myself that by following that approach, I will meet the objective within the timeframe given.

Question 21: How does an autistic person see the world? What do you see first when looking at something?

An autistic person sees the world like anyone else really. How they interpret it is something different entirely.

Anabella and Sally explain that they focus on two points – the start point and the end point. Their focus shifts and moves from one place to another. Point A will be extremely detailed and point B will be equally detailed. They can see them as clear as anything, every line, every shade and in ultra-high definition as well. However, the route from A to B is blurry, like a short-sighted person who takes off their glasses. They can't see past their arm and it is so blurry that even colours merge.

Anabella explains that to help her with this route issue, she positions objects in set places around her desk, her house, and her room. She positions herself around things. Some things are purely there as a break, like a bright new tennis ball or a lamp. Something to break the blurriness and bring point B closer. Sally does similar things with objects at work. Her phone, her pen, pads and even a stapler are positioned so she knows where everything is without looking.

The group may struggle with things when they are moving from one point to another. However, the amazing thing which seems counterproductive, is their ability to notice every small detail around them. When they are looking around, just focusing and their mind is working overtime as usual, then they notice every small pattern on the wall, the lines of the cupboards, the lines on the pad and even when something is slightly not straight.

Question 22: Do you have many friends?

Some of the group explained that they have very few friends. Some even said that they have no friends really. They have a few people that they know but struggle to let inside enough to be considered a friend. Sometimes, someone they thought was a friend questions why they have behaved or reacted a certain way and clearly don't understand them.

Few of the group are extremely happy with the few friends that they have. Some are really close, and they feel 100% safe regardless, and others say they still mask a little but not fully. It is a very long and slow process to build up trust in someone over their autistic traits.

Others have few friends at work and therefore find it difficult to socialise at work gatherings such as the Christmas party. They sometimes feel like they should go to these events, but end up being in the corner and give off a 'do not approach me' vibe until someone they trust comes to them. They are not always able to open up on their own. They wait for a 'safe' friend or colleague to bring them into the conversation and environment. Even with the support of a friend, the trust can take a while to happen. Sometimes it can be very quick or even not at all for the entire event.

Situations around meeting people and starting new relationships are completely situation driven, as well as the company they are in. However, all agree that work situations are the worst and the biggest challenge they face.

Question 23: Would you say your primary/secondary school days were good or a bad experience?

Sadly, most of the experiences that the group had in regard to primary school and some of secondary school was not good. In fact, bad would have been an improvement; some of the experiences were terrible, mine included.

Most of the group explained that they were bullied at school. Bullying is a major issue and the severity of it varies from one member of the group to another. Some of the group do not remember details around primary school but they do remember that they were not happy there and felt like they did not belong. Some knew that they were autistic at primary school, most did not.

Anabella explains that at primary school, she was a loner, having maybe one or two friends. She was bullied severely, verbally, and physically. The school during the infant and early junior stages (years 1 to 4) did not really do anything. The school did not believe it was as bad as Anabella believed it was, even with her mum and I challenging them as much as possible. She still struggled to make friends and did not understand why others treated her the way they did. She was diagnosed with 'moderately severe ASD' and ADHD in year 5.

She is enjoying secondary school so much more. Only four other children from her class went to this school and due to the nature and dynamics of a secondary school environment compared to a primary school one, coupled with the different abilities of the children, she is hardly ever in touch with any of them. She still struggles at secondary school, but she is much better and the experience is better overall. She explains that she was still bullied when in year 7 but she did not allow them to win this time round.

Sally moved secondary schools a lot until she was finally settled. One of the schools was generally good; it was not great and had issues but was OK. This was for a year between the ages of twelve and thirteen. The next school was really bad. The worst experiences she could imagine. Bullying was at a new level at that school and this lasted over a year. Eventually she left and went to a boarding school. This was her best school; however, she was fifteen at the time and coming up to her GCSEs. She was far behind and had a lot of work to do in a very short space of time.

She explained that the boarding school environment was one in which some tolerance was given to the fact that she was autistic and had ADHD as well. However, they still enforced socially acceptable behaviours and gave lessons, learning from situations in which they may have done something inappropriate. Sally said that these lessons were extremely valuable and helped her immensely. These were not done at the previous schools and she believes that all schools should have these lessons to help all children, regardless of a disability.

Question 24: Do you think the school did enough to help and support you?

They did well in some areas and in other areas could have been better, but some of the earlier schools were completely ignorant and clueless over autism and had no idea what to do. I can state that the working environment is the same. Some places I have worked were better in one area and failed, on a whole new level, in other areas. You could say the same about schools for children without any disabilities – that there are always areas that could be better. The key is for those areas of concern to be reviewed and learnt from. Sadly, not all do.

Michael and Sally went to boarding school so experienced a different environment to the others. The majority of the group did not understand some of the areas of schooling. The support was there but was not enough for them. They seemed to get into more trouble or were told off for reasons that they could not always understand and most of the time there was not an explanation.

Sally explained that the house parents at her school could have done better but they were learning just as she was. But the teachers and staff knew how to control the children. The children had fun, they laughed and enjoyed lessons. They learnt in interactive sessions, the school was very inclusive and they knew how to keep the levels of engagement high. One of the ways that they taught was very visually, which Sally hated when she was younger. However, she recognises now that it made such an impression that she uses it as a way of turning situations and problems into a visual diagram which allow her to find a resolution.

The school's biggest asset was the fact that these children, who were extremely scared of being labelled as a weirdo, were able to be themselves. They were not made to feel silly for being different. It made such a huge impact on her confidence. She believes that without those years, she would not be the lady she is today.

Question 25: How important were your parent(s) help and support?

Parents always try to be the best that they can for their children. Unfortunately, what they think is best, does not always help. It is something that parents struggle with over their children, regardless of any disability. I can definitely agree to that statement.

My upbringing was very difficult. I came from a broken home, having only a mother with stepbrothers and sisters. They have always been my brothers and sisters. The step part has never and will never be a thing in our household. There is a massive age gap between me and my older brothers; they left home when I was a teenager. There is also a gap with my younger sisters, so I felt odd within the family. As I had no dad, I struggled to find an identity for a long time. My biological dad left around six months before I was even born. My stepdad and I did not have a great relationship. I never really got any support, from my mother or anyone else in my life; I did it all by myself. I talk openly about how all of that impacted me, mainly negatively in my early years. However, during my late twenties I have accepted it, learnt from it, and have since been helping others learn from my experiences.

Sally explained that she had a big dislike of her parents from the ages of fifteen to eighteen. Some of that will be the typical teenager growing up, those years just before being an adult, but she felt that she did not get any help or support during those difficult years after being diagnosed. Their approach was to show by actions rather than words. For this group, this is very difficult as they need to understand and engage. Therefore, the impression given is that they are lazy and that is not the case.

One of her examples was about a time when she was seventeen. She went out with her friends, got very drunk and stayed out all night. She left the house around 9 p.m. and ended up coming home after 6 a.m. the following morning. As a result of that night, she was deemed irresponsible and was treated as such until she was twenty-one.

Now the relationship is not like that at all. She is now in her early to mid-twenties and she turns to her mum for nearly everything. She lives in London, goes back home at least twice a month and will regularly seek advice from her mum. She also has a special relationship with her sister; she is the one person that she trusts implicitly.

Question 26: Does anyone else in your family have a disability?

Some of the group have family members with other disabilities or who are also autistic. Anabella, my eldest daughter, and I are both autistic. Others have autistic siblings who have ADHD too. Other members believe that they have either parents or grandparents that are potentially autistic or at least have a number of autistic traits. However, they have not been diagnosed.

One of the group explained that she believes that both of her grandparents were autistic, as her nan was very averse to change, extremely set in her ways and did not like her routine being disturbed at all. Her granddad worked at NATO and was extremely technical, so much so that he seemed to be at a different level compared to his peers.

Question 27: When was the lowest point in your life and what happened?

Some of the group have had some extremely low points in their lives. Some, unfortunately, have thought about suicide and some have even acted upon those thoughts. The mental health of a person is extremely important and there needs to be better support for society in general. I have been an advocate of mental health for a number of years; it is great to see that is it now slowly being understood better with improved support. There is still a way to go. When you are deemed as 'awkward' or 'different' to your peers and society gives the impression that you are less than everyone else, then mental health and support becomes an even more important issue.

Some of the group suffer with extreme anxiety and have struggled quite badly. Some have suffered due to external factors, others when they decided to come off their medication or when moving away from home. The change from university, learning and the routine of this environment to one of working life and a whole new routine can be very stressful. Some of the group were part of an autistic internship programme for a large international financial company. One still pinches herself that she had that role within the bank; she does not believe that she deserves this in terms of her own place and independence. She is extremely hard on herself, which is quite common within the group, but she does deserve everything she has. She has worked extremely hard and battled a number of challenges, both inside and out, and has overcome so much.

Some of the group have a few difficult months every year when they have a wobble, caused by a variety of situations. Some of the group have lost family and friends. They explain that they were really close to them and how they struggled to process the fact that one morning the person was alive and then later that evening they were not. They were unable to talk with them, unable to see them and hold their hand like they had previously done.

One of the older members of the group explained that he has struggled with mental health for a number of years for lots of different reasons. Some of them are life events that have taken place and put him in some very dark places. He was depressed and on medication and even acted upon suicidal thoughts. He explains that his mental health is like a giant yo-yo or rollercoaster; when he is happy then it is like being on a cloud but when he is down then he is extremely depressed, suicidal and struggles to carry on. The lowest point was knowing that he needed support but was unable to get it.

Question 28: You seem really happy and cheerful, is this an act?

Of course, it is most definitely an act. The majority of what you see every day is an act.

These words, or similar, were expressed by nearly all of the group. The reasons for the 'faking it to make it' is, however, very different for each of them.

Some of the group explain that being positive all the time, even when you do not feel it, helps calm them and stops them reacting as much. It gives them confidence or belief that they can control a lot of their autistic traits. Others act cheerful so it saves them from the difficult conversations around explaining that they are autistic or other reactions to this.

Others are much older and say that being down, depressed or not trying to be positive has no benefit. To anyone, not themselves or anyone else around them so why bring everyone else down. I try to stay as positive as possible, even if some days are completely faking it. Everyone has bad days; some have bad weeks or even months. A situation like a death of a family member or close friend can make the happiest person down. Mental health is so important and even the pretence of acting happy can have a positive effect and sometimes, you need to act happy just to stop you crying and get through the day.

Question 29: Outside of either school/work or home, what other support do you have?

A lot of the group do not have outside support. Some have outside activities like sporting groups such as playing football, but they do not join the social evenings outside of match day.

Some of the group have become friends with people that supported them during work and school. One lady had a mentor who has now become a close friend to her. They explain that the majority of them find it difficult to join the groups as they have no other autistics to relate to or anyone to build that safe person relationship with – the one person that can understand them a little better and allows them to not feel like a lesser person when one of their traits become too much.

Anabella and I both have our own routines. We tend to shut ourselves away from each other and the outside world so we can relax and listen to music or express ourselves in a way which does not draw looks from people out in public.

Question 30: What do you want to do when you leave school/university? What is your ideal career?

Anabella expressed a passion for what she would like to do; she wishes to become either an actress or a fashion designer. She explained that she loves the idea of being different people, pretending to be someone else and acting differently to how she normally does. In drama school, she struggles to understand concepts and get facial expressions right. She says that her drama lessons have been massive in helping her confidence and learning the reactions of others.

Sally said she wanted to be a detective or work in counter terrorism doing analysis. She explained that the puzzle element of those roles, of putting things together in an order and by a set time, is one of the main thrills of the job. She enjoys the investigation stage of finding the issue or being given a problem and working out how to fix it. Then the execution stage of implementing the resolution, documenting what you have done and processing it to conclusion.

Question 31: Do you think it is fair that the world believes that you will not be able to do anything and never amount to anything because you're autistic?

No, it is appalling to teach people that they will never amount to anything. It is demoralising if, when you explain to someone that you are autistic, their reply is "I'm sorry".

A lot of the group, especially the eldest members, remember teachers, friends and even family saying that they would not amount to anything and they had to just do what they could. There was no belief that they could get a good job or be successful. The elder members explained that they had very few, if any, autistic people to be inspired by, as opposed to now where there are autistic actors, directors, and writers as well as some who are publicly open about their autism in well-known companies.

Anabella and some of the younger generation explained that their parents, as well as themselves, refused to believe that they could not do anything. They were told that they were strong; they could achieve whatever they set out to. It would be extremely hard but they knew that if they wanted it and worked hard enough for it then they could do it. They also had role models who got A* in GCSEs and so tried to emulate them.

Sally hated the idea that at thirteen, she felt that her life was meant to be mapped out. That if she did not have an idea at that stage of her life, then she would fail. I teach my girls that their GCSEs are a stepping stone to having choices. The better GCSEs you have then the more choices you have available to you. You do not have to know what you want to do at that stage, but you should give yourself the chance to do it once you know. Autism is a scale; some will face more difficulties than others. That is no different to two non-autistic children of the same age struggling in different subjects at school or even different areas within the same subject lesson.

Society and the media are changing their attitude towards autism; until recently, the news was always about of one end of the spectrum. They would report on someone non-verbal or with severe learning difficulties who would struggle to get any qualifications. Even an autistic person at the opposite end of the media scale was told this would be difficult. They should prepare themselves to do nothing more than working in the warehouse of a supermarket. How narrow-minded people are to think that. Plus, what is wrong with working in a warehouse?

Members of this group have got degrees in Business and achieved a 1:1; others have psychology degrees and even degrees specialising in Autism. Three of us work for a large international financial company at one of the country's head offices. We are not just counting computer monitors which the media would portray is all we can do. Others, such as me, did not get A-levels or go to university but I am an author and have worked within financial services for over fifteen years specialising in Reward and Compensation at senior levels.

The UK workforce is comprised of approximately 16% autistic people. These are the ones who have either declared this to their companies or and have been diagnosed and recognised by the government. There will be a number of adults working who are not diagnosed too. Many seem to believe that 'achievement' is based on your role and the amount of money you earn. The more degrees you have, the more money you will earn, this means you are more important and therefore you have achieved something. Personally, I strongly disagree with that statement. The builder who built my house, on average earns half of what a Project Manager earns. Does this mean he is half as skilled as me? Am I worth twice as much as he is? Of course not – it is totally absurd to even think like that. He is skilled in a different way to me. I cannot build a house and have no idea how to; he does.

Question 32: What do you think others need to learn about autistic people like yourself?

Firstly, don't assume that you know everything about all autistic people, or anything for that matter. Even if you actually know an autistic person, we are not all the same. Just the same as a neurotypical person is not the same as every other neurotypical person.

Autism traits and the reactions that an autistic person may have can come across as being stroppy. However, this is not the case at all. Autistic people find it so frustrating that they cannot explain why they react in the way that they do. They are struggling to process information or are unable to explain something to you in a way that you may understand.

The same way that a neurotypical person learns about others or a new job, it is a learning curve. Things may need to be explained more than once. A person should not be judged on one reaction or by one mistake. People should try to be understanding, are polite and more importantly, educate that person. An autistic person works the same way. We are learning a new role/skill and therefore we require some level of understanding and tolerance, and an explanation when we do not understand something, even if it seems to be the simplest concept.

Think about the game show Who wants to be a Millionaire? The concept was classed as silly when it was first introduced; answer fifteen questions and win one million pounds. Very easy, if you know the answers to the questions; not so easy if you don't. Remember – you may know the answer to one of these fifteen questions that I don't, but I may also know an answer to another question that you don't.

Treat others how you would wish to be treated.

Question 33: Do people believe that you are autistic when you tell them?

Never – even family members refused to believe this initially. Some of the group understand why others do not believe that they are autistic. It seems that there is a stereotype for every race and equality.

The media need to take responsibility for the impact that they have on society. The media is not held to account and are either unaware of the influence and damage that they can cause or are wilfully ignorant and uncaring. Either way it helps feed the fire than put them out. Some may argue that they show what society is feeling, and to a point they are. However, the group feel that it is more the other way around when it comes to autistic people such as themselves.

If a gay person told you that they were gay, you would not tell them they are not or that they do not look gay. You would not tell a black person that they are not black either. It is offensive, very insensitive, even belittling to someone else by responding in that manner. Why tell an autistic person that they are not autistic?

Question 34: Do you think that all autistic children should be kept together rather than interacting with other children?

Should we go back to the days of segregation? Should white people and black people be separated like back in 1960's America? Should all gay people be put together? Is it acceptable to do this with autistic people?

Keeping autistic people apart from non-autistics does not allow them to develop and function in society and equally does not develop an understanding and acceptance within society of autistic people, and other disabilities as well. The only way that society and people can work together is by interacting; by developing an understanding, acceptance, and knowledge of each other. In short – To be able to work together, you need to be together. History has shown that when you divide groups, it creates resentment and problems arise. Integration is key to developing society, a society for all. Inclusion is a word used a lot and with very good reason.

I, along with others within this group, recognise that due to the scale of the spectrum, some autistic people are dependent on others and, therefore, going to a school which is specially designed to cater for their needs would be the best for them. However, the majority of others benefit more from support within society to be the best that they can be with the challenges that this condition has given them.

Question 35: Do you feel limited by your disability?

Sally explained that she feels 100% limited by her disability – not just her autism and ADHD but also by the fact that she is a woman; at least with her autism, she has developed techniques to mask it. Working situations are stressful. Events such as formal meetings where she may have to shake hands are a challenge for her. What is the correct protocol for different circumstances? Sally and others, including myself, struggle with this: a social work event compared to a formal one; how you should interact with your colleagues; is there a difference in the way you address your peer group compared to those senior to you? And if so, why?

Sally finds it a struggle to work out what society's rules are on this subject. She sees how some people seem to work the room effortlessly but is not sure how they manage to do this. She does, what she believes is, the same as others but obtains a different reaction and is unable to process the differences.

Question 36: How are you finding your first job after school / university?

Michael and Sally left university recently and gained a place on an autistic internship programme. Autistic people give a different perspective to a company because of how they see the world and interact within it. I personally would like to see these programmes expanded. This is one of the main reasons why I founded (dis)Ability and Inclusion – to help companies expand their existing services and get the best talent.

Michael, Sally and Stephan have now completed the three-month internship programme they got onto after graduating. All of them have either been extended as a contractor or have been made permanent within that company. This is great news for them and the financial services company that ran the internship programme.

Sally did not have a great start in the programme. She explained that she liked her manager but not the team. They were not very responsive and did not want to interact with her, despite her efforts. They seemed to make comments and wait for her to explode or have a meltdown. She felt they were watching out for the first time that she did something that she was told not to and then seemed happy to tell her that she had made a mistake.

Perhaps the team had pre-conceived ideas about autistic people or the fact that the interns were only there for three months. Maybe the team members did not want to develop a relationship with someone over a short period of time. Whatever the reason, it is not a good start for anyone to be treated in this way, regardless of whether they are autistic or not.

The treatment from the team was very much like some of the media treatment of Gretta Thunberg when she made the climate change talk to the UK parliament. There were many comments on Twitter asking for her, a child, to be harshly interviewed and perhaps have a meltdown on public television. This cowardly and disgusting behaviour was shown by elected members of the UK parliament. The same people, who are meant to be adults, are responsible for running our country.

After the internship, Sally applied for other jobs within the bank and after interviews, she got a role within the finance team. She now enjoys working with the team; it is full of men but Sally feels that men are more like her, in that they are straight talking and upfront. Her experience of working with women is that they tend to be the opposite. As an autistic person, she is very direct and upfront, so it works well for her.

Michael explained that in one instance, they moved about twenty people in the team around for him as they thought this would make things easier for him. However, it did not take away some of the sensory issues that were happening. He felt bad about raising it as the whole team had moved for him and so he found himself in a difficult position. Members of the team realised that he was not staying at his desk for very long and therefore asked if the new desk was OK. He explained that it wasn't but he did not want to raise it as it would upset the team, having to move again because of him. He was told not to worry about upsetting someone; if he is not comfortable then he is not the best that he can be, so it benefits everyone in the team.

Question 37: Why do you obsess over Harry Potter? Do you understand that it is not real?

Anabella has a fascination with Harry Potter. She explained that she understands that it is not real now, although when she was younger she did not. She believed it was real and that she was going to Hogwarts School of Witchcraft and Wizardry when she received the letter for her birthday. Just like Harry did.

Now she is a little older, it is still a story which she can relate to – the outcast child, not liked and struggles to fit in with others. She thinks that this is no longer an obsession as it used to be, but Harry Potter will always have a special place with her.

Question 38: What do you think schools / universities can do more to help other autistic students?

From an education point of view – listen and stop making assumptions that they know what is best. Never assume anything.

Sally explained that assumptions were made about her before even meeting her for two main reasons: because she is female and because she has ADHD and autism. After meeting her, people realise that she does not behave how they thought she would. We need to focus on the diagnosis and how best to help the person by listening to them (as they know better than anyone else), but we must be patient as they may have trouble explaining what they need.

The biggest and most difficult talks and experiences seem to be with specialists (or so-called specialists): someone who thinks they know autism well but ends up not listening to the person and keeps pushing for what they think is best. I have experienced this over many years, including former managers who thought they knew better with little or no experience, neither of autism or me as a person as they had only been my manager for three months or less. They need to work with the student, listen and try different techniques to see if they work. The school may have resources or techniques which are valid. Both parties need to be open to try things.

Bullying is a big issue that needs resolving for all. Sadly, it is something that nearly all autistic people experience. An example of how a school thought they were helping but actually weren't listening was this incident. To support Sally, the specialist recommended that the school have a teacher escort Sally to the dining hall. This did not work; it did the opposite. It highlighted her as even more vulnerable and different to the rest of the children. The result – the bullying increased the moment the teacher left. When this was brought to the specialist's attention, it was suggested that it would take time before it got better, and that the escort service should remain in place. Specialists need to listen and work with the student to address the underlying issue, be pro-active when possible and not just reactive. Autistic people feel isolated and different at the best of times and the last thing they want is to be paraded as different in front of others. They want to interact and socialise like everyone else; they just find it harder to do.

Another example given by Sally was when she got into a school on a scholarship programme. During one of the learning support sessions, the teacher asked her to colour in a picture of a face with the emotion she was feeling. She was fourteen at the time and she was not sure why she could not explain using words how she was feeling. She tried but was told to colour in the picture. Anabella explained that colouring in a picture was part of her autism diagnosis assessment when she was nine; she was not sure what the colouring in showed the specialist. Some of the group had private education. They said that in terms of support, it would never work until it was recognised and, more importantly, acknowledge that disabilities exist in that environment.

Question 39: What is the best part of being autistic?

Initially, most of the group had a blank look when thinking about this question, but the majority agreed that the best part is how they see the world and the inner strength that they have had to develop. They can't explain in words this inner strength that they have, this resilience, but they are able to push themselves and feel very proud and pleased when they prove a lot of people wrong.

For the majority of their childhood and early into their working careers, they were told that they couldn't do this, couldn't do that. They were told that they couldn't get good grades either at GCSEs or A-levels, and that they would struggle to get a job let alone a high paying one. Everything that was ever said to this group was mainly negative. Often, the more people say you can't do something, the more you believe it, but this group refuse to believe that.

Question 40: Do you regularly have panic attacks or meltdowns?

"Panic attacks – yes, on a regular basis and the majority of them are linked to sensory issues," replied Sally. It could be a result of being in a new place and therefore feeling unsure. Or it could be a change to a known place; it may be louder, or perhaps the decorations or layout inside have changed which affects the sensory input.

Sally and I sometimes have something called a shutdown which is a lesser version of a meltdown; shutdowns are more frequent. Sally used to have a shutdown most evenings after a day of work. She needed quiet time alone, not socialising with anyone, including her partner or family members.

Shutdowns are a recharging process, especially after a day where a lot of concentration has been required. From leaving the house, getting to work, finding the train busier than usual and trying to ensure that they don't have a panic attack, then getting to work and starting for the day. The rare occasion on which a train inspector gets on the train and asks to see their ticket but they had not seen them in advance. When the inspector appears suddenly and beside them, it throws them out of their stride.

Michael explains that he has meltdowns on a regular basis, maybe twice a month on average. Others, like Sally, maybe have one every two or three years. Meltdowns, as described by Sally, are like going back to being four years old and screaming and hiding behind the sofa – the uncontrollable childish behaviour that you see when you take a biscuit from a four-month-old baby. The reason behind the meltdown may not just be one thing; it could be a result of not processing issues, allowing them to build up until they are released somehow. Imagine a water bottle, filled up little by little with an issue. Instead of dealing with that issue on a regular basis, the bottle fills up until its full and then it has to overflow; there is no space left.

The main key trigger seems to be centred around listening. A lot of the shutdowns and meltdowns involve communication, or lack of it. Those who have these meltdowns and shutdowns feel that they are not being listened to during the incident. They believe that the other person is not trying. This goes back to the idea of being called selfish and not trying when they really are. But it works both ways. They do find it increasingly difficult to explain the point that they are trying to make and when they feel the other person is not listening, then they struggle even more to explain. They get frustrated and their emotions increase. The ability to listen and process the discussion is diminished, sometimes to the point of being non-existent. They are unable to progress the conversation and then the meltdown happens, or this episode goes into their water bottle.

It can also happen the other way. Sally said she tried to end a conversation with someone when they reached an impasse. Unfortunately, the other person kept talking, trying to keep the conversation going. The person even followed Sally when she walked away. The situation was continuing with no progress or resolution. Then the meltdown happened.

Question 41: What makes you happy?

"Food," Sally laughed. There was no hesitation; she says she is a self-confessed foodie. She loves food and is not the stereotypical autistic person about food. I am that stereotype as I have approximately ten, maybe twelve, different meals that I will eat and nothing else. I know what I like to eat and therefore this is what I will eat. Previously, I had no interest in trying new food. However, I have got better and will now try new food (as long as it has ingredients that I like). I also need to be in the right frame of mind towards it. I require lots of notice if going to a new restaurant and need to see the menu in advance. I cannot do it as a spontaneous lunch or dinner that evening.

All of us acknowledge that our friends make us happy. We are all cheerful people and enjoy spending time with those that we feel comfortable around and some are glad that they do not have to work as hard as they normally do to mask their behaviours.

Others in the group love animals as well. Some have family pets and Anabella explains that our dog seems to know when either one of us is having a good or bad day. Anabella enjoys it when her dog, Lottie, just comes and sits next to her. Lottie rests her head on Anabella's legs for the whole night. Anabella feels safe when Lottie does that; she can just relax, feel a lot calmer and slowly stroke her dog. She remains still until she feels better. I've been told that anxiety dogs apply pressure on the person to make them feel grounded. They feel this weight on them and this helps calm them down. Once Lottie feels that Anabella is calmer, she jumps off and goes and grabs a toy for playing. Lottie's way of asking if everything is OK now. Anabella always feels better after playing with the dog.

Question 42: Do you have any clubs or organisations that you are involved in?

Some of the group shake their heads viciously. No. They absolutely hate the first day or the first introduction of joining a new club, so much so that now some of the group will not join any new clubs at all.

Sally and Anabella explain that they really want to join some clubs and build on their very small social circle. The issue is that they struggle to find any clubs or groups that they feel comfortable in. Sally has spent so long building this safety wall inside her that it takes a long time to break it down and let people in. Most have decided that they avoid this now as it is easier for them.

The risk of this is being isolated. Maybe not now in their twenties and thirties but when they are older or lonely, for whatever reason, they will not have developed those social skills. Human beings are not designed to be isolated, we are a social species, even if it is being social with one person or one activity.

Question 43: Being autistic, you must be a Math Genius?

Believe it or not, not all autistic people are Einstein or a mathematical savant. We are the same as everyone else. We have skills in some areas and not in others. Some of the group are very good at maths, like me, but I would not class myself as a genius. Far from it. Others are amazing at music, but they are not like some of the experts who can listen to a piece of music once and then replay it first time without any mistakes, or even know from the sound what key was played.

Sally explained that she is rubbish at maths. She can do OK, but would not say that she is at a level like others she knows. She did think that she was amazing at art. She loved the colours and experiments in her art lessons along with the different textures and materials used for art. However, she could not deal with chalk: Handling chalk; the sound of chalk on the board or the canvas; and the powder which transferred to her hand. But everything else, she loved. Painting, the strokes of the brushes and even painting using her hands. The other great part of art was the ability to walk around the table, get different things from the classroom and not having to sit still in the chair for an hour.

I loved maths as a subject. During high school, I generally completed the work during the explanation stage of the lesson. It was explained and I understood so I started the work, while the teacher explained it more for the rest of the class. While others were working, the teacher would give harder work for me to do. Maths was logical to me. It is an absolute and by that, I mean that the answer is either right or wrong. The answer to twelve multiplied by twelve is one hundred and forty-four. It will never be anything else; it does not matter which method you use to get the answer it will be one hundred and forty-four and always will be. There is not a grey area like in English lessons. I hated English while at secondary school; I did not enjoy reading and never really knew what people meant when reading texts. Now I am always reading; I generally read a book every week or two.

Question 44: Do you enjoy your own free time?

Without a doubt, I absolutely love it.

All of the group love their own free time. However, some things that they do on their own are not always good experiences.

Sally says that swimming is one of those activities which she finds hard. It is hard for her because of the walking around the pool and changing in and out of swimwear. The biggest difficulty is when people cross lanes in the pool where they seem to appear out of nowhere or she bumps into them. She always struggles with the fact that you can never tell how busy the pool is until you have changed and made your way in there. It could be too busy in which case she would change out of her swimwear and go home instead of even attempting to swim.

Typically, the group like being sociable and being with their friends and family. They enjoy going to the cinema or the park like everyone else. Some of the group like splitting their time equally between their friends and being alone; not being alone because they are overwhelmed (which does happen) but to simply enjoy being alone. I think it is important for everyone to learn to enjoy their own company and being by themselves.

Question 45: What things does an autistic person enjoy?

The same as everyone else. Why would you think otherwise?

We like music, films and being with our friends. We have hobbies like everyone else and each of us is different and therefore have different interests. Some enjoy some stereotypical things such as computer coding or something technical but there will be a number of non-autistic people who enjoy technical activities or computer coding too. We are not keeping it just for ourselves; we share.

BEHAVIOURAL QUESTIONS

Question 1: Why do you make weird faces all the time?

Autistic people do not act in the stereotypical way that most people expect, i.e. they do not sit in the corner rocking, screaming, shouting, jumping around and making silly faces all the time. This is not typical behaviour. Some are not aware of any facial expressions that they may make while others are very aware of some of this.

I have major difficulties understanding my facial expressions and my tone, especially when I am quite animated about a subject. I am reminded a lot about how my face and tone seem to be the complete opposite of the expression of the words which leave my mouth.

The expressions mostly occur during an activity or while thinking; the body and face do things to help them focus. Some have an open mouth while thinking, others clap and the clapping increases in volume and frequency as they process, and their thinking elevates. Others look disconnected and the question is repeated, maybe even repeated twice, as there may be no facial expression at all. They are thinking, then all of a sudden, they blurt out the answer so unexpectedly that they are asked to repeat it.

Facial expressions could also be a reaction to stress or anxiety about a situation. Sally, Michael, and I have been told on multiple occasions that we look angry or annoyed when someone first meets us. Sally describes herself as having a 'resting bitch face' and regardless of when you see her, that is the first face you will see and the face you get when you talk to her while she processes.

Body language is critical. When communicating, 55% of it is through body language and social cues. Looking unapproachable puts the other person in a defensive frame of mind. Many autistic people struggle to interpret these social cues.

Anabella loves making weird faces. For her, facial expressions are a way of communicating and she enjoys expressing an emotion or feeling through making a face. She explained that she has always found it very difficult to express her emotions verbally and therefore will create a range of different faces to express her emotions visually instead. The issue is that what face she thinks she is showing someone, is not what is being portrayed by them. She has been told by teachers and friends that she also makes faces when she is deep in thought. This is something new that has only just recently been highlighted to her. She finds it fascinating and wants to know the differences that her face makes consciously to what is being perceived as well as unconsciously during times of concentration.

Question 2: Why do you talk so loudly?

Some of the group are aware that they talk really loudly and the reason for the increase in volume is dependent on the situation or an emotion. Like anyone else, if you are excited then your pitch increases just like when you are upset or angry.

Stephan explains that his voice gets louder, in anticipation of an event. If he is planning a social event such as meeting friends in the pub, then he already believes that it will be busy and noisy. Therefore, he feels that he will need to speak louder to be heard. He prepares himself for that and walks into the pub speaking loudly from the outset.

A thought which was echoed by a number of the group as a reason for talking loudly is so that they can hear their own voice. This helps them with their thought processes. They feel that if they are unable to hear their own voice then neither can anyone else.

I can relate to that. I remember when I started work and got my very first promotion at eighteen, I was required to give a presentation to my senior management team. I was so nervous and anxious that my voice was really loud, even though I could barely hear myself. My managing director told me after thirty seconds that I did not need to shout as we were all in the same room and not in the warehouse. As a result, I always try now to consciously think about the volume of my voice.

Michael explained that during his secondary school years, voice control was near non-existent for him. He had to learn to focus on his loud voice. He spent ages trying to work on lowering the volume when speaking. The key driver for this was to fit in with school. He did not want to be known as the child that shouts out in class and worked hard to develop those same social skills as others. This enabled him to be a part of the class. He was included and accepted as opposed to being the outsider and pushed aside. When you meet someone who is loud and shouts, you probably think that they are rude or obnoxious, maybe even selfish, and no one wants to be thought of as those things. An autistic person is even more sensitive about these things. They try harder than anyone to fit in with others, maybe a little too hard, and sometimes they feel it is not enough. Perhaps this is because they are told it more frequently, or they become frustrated that everyone else seems to pick up these social behaviours quicker and easier than they do. Maybe they notice the negative reactions from others when they do it.

Anabella states that she has no control over her voice. It is very difficult for her to control the volume. Even during a sentence, the volume can range which can be difficult for others to focus on the words and follow what she is talking about. She is working very hard on controlling her volume by creating different situations to practise in. She loves reading out loud to her younger sisters – when she reads, this ability is amazing to hear and makes me stop while I'm working to listen to the story as it's gripping. I hope she does not learn to control it too much.

The rest of the group explained that their voice control seems to be limited and harder to manage when they are discussing something that they are extremely passionate about. They become more expressive and this can last a few sentences or for the rest of the conversation.

Question 3: Why do you talk in a weird voice? You sound like a young child?

Sally explains that she is not often loud, but her voice does change into a different accent on certain words. While living in Thailand, she met a group of Irish girls and as a result when the word 'grand' is used, that word is said with an Irish accent. It is a heavy Irish accent too. Autistic people can and do imitate words, phrases or even actions which they see and hear. Once they do, it potentially stays with them forever – their brain translates that this is the way to say or do it. Children pick up on phrases from parents and others they interact with on a long and regular basis. If you have children, I am sure that you have seen them act out your mannerisms, repeat your phrases in the same way that you do. If this happens in public, you may have got comments such as, 'clearly your child' or something similar. I know I have with all three of mine for different things that they do.

Some of the autistic traits that manifest themselves are a result of anxiety or stress, happiness, or excitement. These traits may be magnified or more exaggerated when in a heightened state. Other traits, such as the Irish accent for a particular word, is just that. If the brain processes that a particular word should be pronounced with that accent, then just like $1+1 = 2$, this will always be the answer. Sally's brain states that 'grand' should be spoken with an Irish accent and there is nothing she can do to change it

Michael is another person who also seems to have an accent which appears when excited. He was born in the South of England and went to university in the North of England. Spending a number of years there resulted in listening and speaking with a northern accent at times. Mainly when he was excited. He was asked while at university why he spoke with a northern accent; it was the same as trying to control the volume of his voice. He wanted to fit in with everyone. He wanted to fit in with the environment and the people. In his case, the university and the students and friends he made there. His brain was consistently saying that this was the way to do it and therefore the brain processed this accordingly.

Stephan expressed that his voice does not change, regardless of any word or state of mind, but only in volume. The louder he becomes, the more heightened state he seems to be in.

Anabella is younger than the others in the group by over ten years and she explained that she creates weird faces for expressing things as well as her using her voice. She is a teenager but is not very tall and therefore does not look her age. She is often treated like a younger version of herself. She likes her younger voice, which is slightly baby-fied, as a way of playing up to the image that others have pictured of her. It works well for her when she plays up, but has an adverse effect as when more mature activities are on offer or mature students are required, she is overlooked almost instantly.

Question 4: Why do you ask the same question over and over again?

"Because I forget. I get distracted easily from one activity to the next," replied Anabella. Repeating the same question allows someone to stay focused on the task at hand. Anabella finds that it helps her to process her response.

Some autistic people struggle with change or a new setting. Some questions are asked over again due to the environmental change around them. For example, going to a new place to meet a group of friends or even strangers, such as a new social group or activity class. The change of venue is the difficulty and can cause anxiety leading up to the event. If they are very anxious, a person may end up not going to the event. They may feel unprepared or have repeated questions which they have been unable to process and retain the answers given.

Sally explains that she will keep asking the same question in preparation for that day. So, when she went away with some friends for a weekend, she had a key person within the group who she kept asking questions of. – Questions such as what time they were leaving and where were they all meeting. She would ask over and over again in the days leading up to the day they were going away to make sure that the plan of activities was embedded.

Others, such as Anabella, do not have a concept of time. Anabella finds she can have her expectations set at the beginning of the day, but when she gets home, she will ask questions for the next activity or event, including dinner. A common event in our household is when she asks when dinner will be. If she is told dinner will be approximately five minutes, she will ask again in two minutes, then two minutes after that and keep asking until dinner is ready. If a timeframe is not known and she asks if she can play a game, then her expectation is that dinner will take place after her activity finishes. If dinner arrives before then she gets confused and anxious. She thinks that she has been bad and not being allowed to play her game is a consequence for something she has done.

Stephan explained that he does not repeat the question because he is distracted or because he is anxious, he does it because it is part of his response and he just needs to. His brain translates a question in the same way that you were told to do a maths question at school – write down the question, the workings out and the answer so you can check it. He is the same; he needs to repeat the question before responding with the answer. It keeps him in the moment. Anabella said that repeating the question creates more time for her to process, so the other person knows she has heard the question and is trying to work it out.

Sally said when she was asked questions when she was younger, she was very still. There was no movement or acknowledgment that she had heard the question. As a result, people kept repeating the question, believing that she had not heard or understood it. This, unfortunately, distracted her and made her lose her train of thought. She had to start all over again to formulate her response. She started repeating the question, just like Anabella, as a way to show the person she had heard which gave her more time to process without any distraction and then respond.

Others within the group keep saying yes, and/or nodding, or any other variation to show that they are paying attention. The reality is that the majority of these responses are automatic. When someone says hello, you say hello back and 'how are you?' When someone is leaving, you say goodbye and 'have a good evening'.

I myself ask almost everyone that I communicate with on a Monday the same standard message. Hello, how are you? I hope you had a good weekend. Friends respond with what they did, usually talking about meeting friends or going out for dinner. My automatic reply is as standard as my question – "That sounds like a great weekend and the food sounds nice." I hate to admit it, but I have zero interest in the dinner as I am extremely limited with my food intake.

I am quite a direct person and ask questions to which I require an answer. As I have got older and more senior within my career, others who know me well comment that I don't say 'hello' or 'how has your day been?' first. I always do this as a response, as though I am not interested or don't care. This is not strictly true. I am interested in how others are and generally care if they are struggling but the idea of small talk and asking these things is like a different language. I struggle to process and make it work.

I now work very hard to develop the skills to express an interest which can be seen by others. This is not being fake as I am interested. I now understand more about the idea of engagement with others. Part of that engagement is not just asking someone in another team to look at this piece of work and comment but to explain a bit more and create a relationship with that person. This is what some autistic people struggle with.

Reassurance was another reason given to this question; ensuring that they understand the question before trying to process the answer. Roger and Sally both explained that it was more for their reassurance now that they are older that they fully understand what is being asked of them. As well as reassurance, an autistic person can get anxious too. Getting worked up trying to answer the question, which they believe they should know the answer to.

All the group have explained that sometimes they have misread the body language of the person asking the question, thinking that they are getting bored or expecting the answer quicker. Therefore, they get frustrated and start repeating the question to reignite engagement, otherwise the thought process that they are going through just stops dead.

Michael explained that for him to be able to answer questions or explain something, he paints a picture in his head. He repeats the question to create the different parts of the image in his head, then he can run through the response like a storyboard. The response for me has to follow a logical order.

Question 5: Why do you consistently do things that you are told not to do?

Some of the group are very literal. When told something once then that is the standard set for them, they stick with that. Stephan explains that the idea of doing something that he was told not to do can make him very anxious. He explained that when he was younger, while travelling on a bus, there was a poster asking customers not to eat on the bus. Therefore, he still will not eat on any public transport at all. Bus, train, tube, or even in the back of a taxi car, he will not eat or drink anything.

Others feels that they need to understand why they should not do things. Sally needs to know from a work perspective. She needs to understand why, especially if she thinks that what she wants to do is the right process and can explain it.

Michael does not like being told what to do and what not to do. When he was younger, he was told that he shouldn't clap in public, or behave in a way deemed as inappropriate, because it is not the expected behaviour in society. Even in school, he could not go to the toilet when he needed to go – toilet breaks were at set times. He elaborates that it feels so hard mentally to try and keep on top of his behaviour and conform to social standards and cues, not because he doesn't want to, but because it takes a lot of energy to concentrate and focus for so long. The others in the group echo this and all of them want some control back in their life.

Sally and Anabella explained that they had parents and close relatives who would not allow them to behave with their typical autistic behaviours, such as rocking in a corner or clapping while out of the home. Therefore, they have learnt to mask their behaviour very well. Although physically you do not see the behaviour, mentally they are working extremely hard to keep their body under control. It is said that girls, in general, are better at masking behaviour and copying their peers than boys do. This is one of the reasons why girls seem to be more mature than boys and is potentially a reason why not as many girls are diagnosed as should be.

Anabella explained that she does like to push the boundaries as far as possible and keep going until she gets caught. She knows she is going to get caught and she keeps doing it until that happens. She knows it is wrong to do what her parents have told her not to do, but she keeps going regardless. When she gets caught, she feels incredibly guilty for disobeying her parents and then the circle continues. She feels that she is slowly learning how to control herself more since being at secondary school. She is not sure if this is her just growing up and learning about herself, or learning about her conditions better. She knows she has a lot more work ahead of her.

Question 6: Why do think people treat autistic people as a child regardless of their age?

The media. People with autism are portrayed usually at the worst end of the scale. Majority of the group feel that the media is now even less balanced than before, especially the older generation within the group, and I agree with that thought. I remember when stories used to be balanced; they at least gave you both sides of the argument and let the reader decide. Now, this is much less so and often the headlines are completely biased. The media generally show the stereotypical autistic person that struggles with basic functions, what the media world used to categorise as 'low functioning': usually a person who has little concept of right and wrong and personal boundaries; a person with excessive gestures and often inappropriate social behaviours; a person who does not or is unable to work. This is a subset of people with autism, of course it is, but not all autistic people are like that. Just as not all autistic people are maths geniuses, not all autistics are non-verbal. Autistic people are people just like everyone else. They are different because they see and experience the world differently.

Talking to an adult like they are a child is insulting and condescending. Speaking to an autistic adult as a child is equally not acceptable behaviour. An autistic adult is a person who is intelligent and deserves the respect that any other person in this world does. It is a misinformed assumption about autistic people that they do not understand the 'way of the world'. Therefore, they do not have the intelligence to process things so you have to speak down to them. I saw a video by an MP recently who explained that as a number of disabled people in her constituency have learning difficulties and do not understand money, they do not need as much, and therefore their benefits can be reduced. It is truly shocking that this took place at the end of 2019. The fact of the matter is that those people probably require more money to care and support them. We all hope that the words on these pages help increase awareness and the truth surrounding autistic people.

"Society is not very nice to us," was the response from Anabella. She says that although she acts up and sometimes acts like a child younger than she is, society treats her as an outsider anyway so she might as well do what makes her happy. She never hurts anyone or is mean to anyone. When she tries to be someone else or what society says she should be, she is told she is a fake and should just be her. Just like Sally – she is damned either way.

Question 7: Why does it take you a long time to answer questions?

Some questions are harder than others. Sometimes it is not the question that is taking the time to answer, sometimes it is the environment. There may be too many distractions or the anxiety of someone new asking a question expecting an instant response which is not readily available.

Questions are subjective. A question is simple if you know the answer but difficult if you do not. Very much like the Who wants to be a Millionaire? game. Winning a million pounds is easy if you know the answers to the fifteen questions you are going to be asked. Any question asked requires processing. Michael explained that he tends to rearrange questions from words into pictures in his mind. This allows him to be able to process it and then answer better.

Sally explained that she generally overthinks any question she is given. She tries to anticipate what the objective is as opposed to answering the question. This can lead to frustration and an increase in her anxiety levels. Anabella explained that when asked a personal question, she feels like she will be judged upon answering. This, in turn, leads to her overthinking the question as well and trying to process all the possible outcomes and reactions before answering with the one which she believes will get the least reaction. This is not always the best answer or the most accurate to the question asked.

I remember once I was in HMV looking for DVDs as they had a big sale on. I was struggling to find a certain TV show at the time. I kept walking up and down the aisle. I was wearing a black polo shirt, very similar to what the staff wore but without any HMV logo branding. A lady came up to me so quickly that I did not see her approach and asked me for a specific film. She was very direct, and her tone was short and sharp. I suppose she had been looking for it for a while and was frustrated when she couldn't find it. It was a film that I had not heard of and it sounds like a foreign, potentially subtitled, film. I just stood there. My thought process had been broken – I was systematically going through the shelves looking for my film. I was then having to process this question. I was not staff. I did not look like staff, in my opinion. I was not wearing an ID badge or anything and I wasn't holding DVDs like I was looking to stock the shelves. So, I remained still and silent as I continued to process all of this. She asked again, this time a little more aggressively than before with an extra comment saying that 'as I work here, I should bloody well know'. This time, I was able to process and had a comment that I could respond with. I responded clearly that I did not work here, that she should ask someone who does and went back to my shelf, searching for my DVD. She was not impressed. She huffed and walked away, saying that she would complain about me to the manager. I got no apology or acknowledgement that she was in the wrong with her assumption, which is fine. Everyone makes mistakes.

A little while later, I saw her shouting at someone else, presumably a manager, as he was in a suit. She even pointed at me when she spotted me. I hope he was a manager and not some poor man who was wearing a suit looking for a DVD on his lunch break.

Question 8: Do you avoid having conversations?

Yes, especially if it is a social occasion and/or I am feeling extremely tired. Body language is a key element of conversation and some of the group, such as Sally and Michael, are not really good at reading body language. The difficulty of reading body language is one of the biggest challenges for an autistic person during conversations. Basic body language is understandable once you have been taught it. For example, crossed arms is a sign of being defensive and disengaged; very expressive gestures show a clear passion in the subject, which could be positive or negative; tone is much more difficult to read.

Sally was diagnosed at the age of 14. Up to that point, she had struggled with family, friends, and school. After her diagnosis, she began to take control. In 2008 she heard about an eighteen-step behaviour interaction program which she worked hard at as she did not want to continue the way she was. One of the key events that helped was the transfer to a new school. A new start for her. The school was described as having an excellent balance of teaching, learning and consequences. The children did act a little crazy at times but they did not try to put the children who were box-shaped into a circular hole. With the support that the new school provided, along with delivering consequences when required, Sally was able to focus on herself. She went on to university and graduated. I met her while she was working for a global financial company in Canary Wharf. The value of the support and understanding given to an autistic person should never be underestimated.

Being autistic seems to be extremely tiring. All the group explain that mentally trying to keep up with social cues and expectations is exhausting. After a few days, they need a day in which to hide away, be themselves and rest without having to focus and concentrate so hard. On these down days, some of the group use the time to read, rest and be lazy. Others use the time to be as crazy as possible. They are in a safe environment like their home or parent's home and can do what they want here without any consequences for socially inappropriate behaviour. An autistic person's mind seems to be working at such a speed that even on down days it does not slow down.

Michael and Sally enjoy social events. They want to engage with others, but only those they know and feel safe with. Sally feels that if a new person joins the group then her avoidance kicks in. In terms of holding a conversation, all the group understand the social cues that are taught when you are younger: say hello, how are you?; talk about the weather; the weekend; your evening plans; the general polite 'small talk'. Once that has been completed, they are not sure what to do. Conversations seem to be very stop-start orientated. They don't flow easily. Generally, at this point the urge to avoid and leave can become too strong to resist.

One of the difficulties all members of the group have is engaging in 'small talk'. They feel it is pointless. Everyone asks the same questions and gets the same automatic responses. No one ever seems to say that they are not well. Every weekend seems to be 'good' or 'relaxing'. My weekends have not been relaxing for years with three young daughters and all the weekend activities that we have as individuals or as a family. When I have responded honestly, this either results in more talking which I am not comfortable doing or the person who only asked out of politeness is unsure how to respond so they walk off. The majority of my weekends have been 'good and relaxing' ever since.

Question 9: Why do you look bored and avoid eye contact when someone is speaking to you?

Sally said, "Sometimes for the same reason as you – I want the conversation to end." However, when the person knows I am autistic then they put it down to this and continue the conversation regardless. Social cues are important. Autistic people are told to learn and follow social cues and try to be more socially acceptable or appropriate. Non-autistic people seem to disregard the same social cues when given by an autistic person as they put it down to their disability. I myself tend to avoid eye contact for the majority of the time that I have a conversation, so I can understand how people can be confused.

A number of autistic people struggle with eye contact for varying lengths of time. It could be that it makes them uncomfortable as they feel like they are staring at someone; this is the main reason for me. I feel that I cannot just look and keep eye contact. I'm either staring or looking around. Another reason could be that something else has caught their attention, like a bright light on a camera or someone talking nearby where the volume has increased. It could even be background music. They are still paying attention to you, even if you think they are not.

Sally and I hate having to maintain eye contact. We understand that is a way of ensuring that others feel comfortable and lets them know that we are engaged in the conversation. The reality is that I am still fully engaged while looking around the room. Others are comfortable with eye contact in short bursts. If the anxiety of the eye contact becomes too much, we may try and shift our focus perhaps just past the person so they hopefully know that we are still engaged. An autistic person could have conflicting emotions about this. They may feel anxious because they are potentially struggling to maintain eye contact, but they also don't want to appear rude by turning away.

Michael explains that he focuses on eye contact as he wants to please others and fit in. He does not want to appear rude and therefore he will try to interact as much as possible with others. He finds it difficult if it is too bright or too loud – his concentration levels decrease, and he struggles to maintain eye contact. Michael was taught that the first meeting with someone is important and that people build an impression of him from that first contact. Therefore, he ensures that his handshake is firm and he gives direct eye contact while saying hello. After that, he finds it more difficult to measure.

The majority of the group find it difficult to find a balance between maintaining eye contact and staring at the person, as well as not appearing bored by looking around the room too much. So much energy is used on that first introduction that the energy drops almost instantly afterwards. Anabella and Michael have worked out a technique they can use: they focus on another area, such as their nose, look just past the person, shift their body weight slightly – enough to stop them becoming stressed – while remaining engaged with the person. This allows them to focus on the conversation instead of struggling with staring and their anxiety.

Question 10: What are you interested in? Autistic people can get very obsessed with something specific.

A lot of the group agreed that when they were younger, they were obsessed with different things. Michael explained that he was fascinated by transport, especially planes. He loved the 787 plane in particular and built a model of this plane. The obsession with transport is now not an obsession compared to his younger days, but he still has a huge amount of interest in it. He explains that his obsession has developed over time, from just transport and particularly planes to airlines and the places where you can travel to, especially by plane to other countries. It has expanded further as he has grown up, to benefits of travel such as reward schemes. Air miles are now developing into an obsession. Strangely, Michael cannot stand airports. From the moment he knows that he is heading to an airport, anxiety levels rise and sensory overload is common. Once on the plane he is fine.

Music is key for Sally and me – we always have to have music playing. I spend most of my day working with YouTube playing classical or soft piano music playing in the background. The main reason is that it stops or reduces other distractions, allowing me to focus solely on the task at hand.

Sally explained that one of her obsessions was actually derived from fear. When she was younger, she loved the water. However, she watched a video about sharks and from that moment on, she was obsessed with thinking that there were sharks around whenever she was near water. It took a while to understand that this was not true and now she has overcome her obsession.

Anabella grew up with Harry Potter and became obsessed with the characters, the books, and the films. If you mention the words 'Harry Potter' then she goes back to being a two-year-old child in a sweet shop for the first time. She gets very excited and even during this part of the interview, she was smiling from ear to ear. She also loves drama and has been going to drama school for over six years.

She has a room full of Harry Potter things such as clothes, books and notebooks and her bedroom door has a Platform 9¾ sign. She has been to Harry Potter World and she has wands and even make-up brushes with a Harry Potter theme (which she says she will never use).

Question 11: Autistic people tend to be more sensitive to different stimulus, are you?

Yes. Very much so. Light, sound, and touch seem to be the main stimuli that impact the group. Anabella explained that some of the stimuli stem from specific incidents. When she was younger, she had her hand grabbed and it shocked her. Ever since, she has not let anyone hold her hand and will not shake hands. This has impacted her so much that her primary school considered not allowing her to go on school trips as she was unable to hold another child's hand while walking. It is important that the education sector learns to manage situations such as this better.

Michael and I are consistently stimulated by sound in both a positive and negative way. We both need to have music playing in the background for the majority of the day. While working, the music we listen to stimulates our brains to a higher state, enabling us to focus and work at an effective rate. The negative impact of sound is when we are somewhere such as a pub. The music may start quiet and then increases in volume later in the evening. As more people arrive, noise levels rise too. This stimulates the brain in a negative way, increases our anxiety levels and makes us want to hide away. Michael described the over sensitivity to noise as the equivalent to having over twenty radios on at the same time, with each radio on a different station and some with that terrible static noise.

Some of the members of group try to manage those negative stimuli to allow them to stay in a busy loud pub for longer. Where they would normally hide away, they are now becoming more open and comfortable than before. Sally explained that although she may be able to stay longer, sometimes it is still too much and has to leave.

The group, in general, believe that they have learnt to manage their stimulus overload better as they have got older and do not believe that they have become any more or less sensitive to those stimuli. Anabella and some of the younger members of the group love being around people but tend to leave when the noise level gets too loud; it feels like this happens very quickly and without warning. Anabella feels trapped and becomes anxious. This makes everything seem louder resulting in her feeling even more trapped. She reacts in a defensive manner – fight, flight or freeze mode. She chooses flight.

Some of the group experience physical pain due to stimuli, mainly light. Michael sometimes feels physical pain when he is exposed to artificial bright lights for too long, such as in an office environment. He develops headaches and looking at lights can be painful. He sometimes needs to take himself away from work and sit in a dark room to try to reduce the severity of the pain and ensure that it does not fully develop into a migraine.

Question 12: You seem to react when holding hands with people. Why is that?

"It is not just holding hands – it is touching the person in general." This is one of the responses given by Sally who puts her reaction to touching down to trust. If you are a new person to her, she will not want to touch you. If a handshake does happen then it needs to be a firm solid palm-against-palm handshake, not a limp-wristed, fingers only type. This type of handshake seems to engage her fight or flight mode; she feels uncomfortable with her body reacting as if it is threatened.

Sally explained that as a woman, some people would potentially lean in to give her a kiss on the cheek, rather than putting out their hand to shake hers while introducing themselves. This is something that she definitely does not like, and she reacts by stepping away from the person, increasing the space around her and pushing out her personal space of safety. To allow any form of touching, she would need to feel safe with the person physically as well as emotionally.

Others within the group explain that they are very independent and therefore when holding hands with someone, they are giving away something of themself to the other person. Security, trust, and a part of them is being offered. Some feel a massive rejection if that person does not take their hand in return.

The majority of the group feel more secure with firm touches and grips as opposed to soft grips and light touches. They are not sure exactly why they prefer this, but their brain seems to process that a light touch is a threat and a firm touch is safe.

Anabella cannot explain why she cannot stand holding hands but that it feels weird and uncomfortable to her. She says that some people want to hold her hand tightly, others loosely, but she still feels restricted regardless of how someone does it; she feels that it stops her from going where she wants, when she wants. During a primary school trip she kept letting go of the other child she was partnered with. The teachers kept making her hold hands, even though she was being sensible. It got to the stage where she stepped into the road to get away. The school decided that she was unsafe to walk on a pavement and would not allow her to go on any further school trips.

As you can imagine, this was contested by her mother and I. The school agreed that she was being sensible and safe when walking on her own but that was their rule. I explained that making a child hold hands for the sake of it is not helpful to the child and creates unnecessary risk, as they found out. She could have been placed at the back with the teacher to keep an eye on her. She is very comfortable holding hands with me now. Although it took nearly a year to learn to do it, now holding my hand is something she does to get calm.

She fully understands that there is no logic to her reactions. She gets weird looks from others when she reacts in the way she does. but, as she has said very clearly and more than once, "I don't like it and it's my hand."

Question 13: Do you like your own company?

Yes. Who wouldn't want to be on their own with their own thoughts looking at the world differently to everyone else?

Each member of the group likes their own company and will go off on their own for a while. Some do it to wind down and relax after concentrating all week to 'fit' in. Others because of an event that has happened, such as a new person joining a group so they need some processing time. Anabella said that most of the time she feels like an outsider, an extra, so she drifts away and ends up alone. It is not what she wants. She, and others, want to interact with the rest of the group but even in school, she has got used to working on her own. She admits that she sometimes reads a book at her desk when the rest of the group are working together; she feels like she is getting in the way so she steps back.

Sally went to a boarding school during her secondary years and therefore she grew up with a smaller tight group of friends. The school had large grounds, so she and others were actively encouraged to explore and develop and, more importantly, enjoy their own company.

If they are not comfortable with a situation, some will walk away and perhaps distract themselves by using their mobile phone. I myself always have a book with me and will go off and read if I feel the situation gets overwhelming for me. Others go for a quick walk around the pub or go outside to get fresh air in an effort to reduce the impulse to completely disengage from the activity. However, if it does not work and their brain is still saying 'time to be alone', they will say their goodbyes and walk away.

Most members of the group have intense relationships with people. They have a lot of faith and trust and, most importantly, security within this group. Any change to this dynamic seems to upset them greatly and therefore they do not feel as safe as before. It could be a new person just saying hello briefly before leaving again that could trigger this impulse and it could impact the whole night for them.

All of the group, however, love company. They like their own company and having 'alone time' but they would rather be with their friends and socialising with others. None of them prefer being on their own; it is more that social interactions for too long or in situations whereby they do not have their very small and tight group of friends, makes it difficult for them to process. It could also be the surroundings, such as loud music or bright lights. They feel the need to escape and be on their own when this becomes overwhelming.

It is so difficult to teach children to develop socially when they feel like outsiders. As a society, I believe that we should be developing independence in our children. Part of that journey is learning from mistakes, social conflicts, and handling those situations independently. However, there needs to be more than leaving those on the autistic spectrum to work it out for themselves. They need support. Everyone needs support and guidance.

Question 14: Why do you not understand body language and facial expressions?

Because it is hard for me. I believe that now, as I approach forty, I do understand these things a lot better than I did at school and in my early working career. However, my brain still seems to interpret it differently to everyone else. Sally and Michael believe that they are good at reading facial expressions when talking, but not the overall body language of the person and it becomes extremely difficult if they feel that they disagree with the other person. Sally said that she finds it hard to interpret, as the face and body seem to not be aligned. Add the words being spoken and the tone used which may not match the expression either. At which point, the conversation shuts down. She is unable to get past this point as she has not listened to the person who is still talking, unaware of this crisis unfolding in her head.

There seems to be a misunderstanding of body language within the group. It is like a puzzle trying to combine the body language with the words spoken and the tone expressed. If the pieces of the puzzle don't match, it is difficult to understand anything until they do. The conversation appears to continue but the autistic person is still trying to process everything so they do not hear anything from that point.

Others find moments where the words, tone and expressions are short and over quickly therefore it is difficult to process. They may need to go away and replay the event in order to try to make sense of it. This could take an hour or a week. Only then are they able to reply or understand that moment.

Body language, on its own, can also be an issue. Some of the group try to copy the body language that is being expressed. However, if this is ignored by a non-autistic person or deemed to be ignored, then some of the group shut down. Anabella is learning a lot from her drama lessons in school as well as a drama theatre school that she attends at weekends. She is being taught about expressions, but she still struggles to process what she sees compared to what she hears, feels, and what she is told.

The biggest difficulty that the group collectively seem to voice is understanding changes to body language and expressions. Sometimes they say or do something, and they sense a change in the group or person they are communicating with. They are confused by the change, and they feel have a sense that the mood is different to before an 'incident'. They cannot tell how the person is feeling but most of the group seem to retreat if they think the person is angry with them. They are usually unable to work out what the 'incident' was that caused the change and feel that everyone else knows but them.

Question 15: Do you think your social interactions within a group environment have improved over time? Do you use therapy or learn techniques to help you?

They have massively improved. The support I have received which has allowed me to process and understand different situations as I have grown up has been invaluable.

As a child at school, it was hard. Children are constantly pushing boundaries and are not fully aware of themselves, let alone being aware of others, especially someone with autism that struggles with social interactions anyway.

During secondary school, Sally and Michael had support developing their social skills. They engaged with others and when misunderstandings occurred, they revisited those situations to help them understand why it happened and how better to read or react to the situation next time. They learnt self-help techniques to understand when their body and brain wanted to do different things. For example, if anxiety is creeping up, take deep breaths or stop the conversation politely for five minutes to have a walk and come back to it.

The group kept going back to the term 'treat others how you wish to be treated'. They believe that if they were calm, polite, and patient then others would be the same with them. However, this did not always seem to work. The group suggested that it could be the situation, the age of the person, the environment or how engaged you were in a situation.

Some of the group had other techniques to help them socially. Sally explained that she read and watched lots of training videos involving expressions and emotions to help her understand what emotion an expression may reveal.

One school that she attended had a role-play session in which different scenarios were acted out and time was spent teaching the cause and effect, the consequences, and behaviours.

One thing that was highlighted by a number of the group were the tellings off that happened when they were younger. They remembered being told off, by teachers, by other family members and parents, but it was never really explained to them what they had done wrong. They had no help with understanding how to improve or develop what behaviour others expected them to portray. The group expressed that they needed to understand the reason why they shouldn't do or not to do something otherwise they found it hard to process.

Understanding the reasoning behind something is never a bad thing. My role is to understand the existing processes, challenge them and create new processes. To do that, I need to have a reason for doing them. Surely, we should teach this earlier so that children and young adults can explain what they mean and understand others.

Question 16: Do you hate being touched or are there certain areas of your body which are more sensitive to touch?

"Forearms," shouted Sally. Even the thought of someone touching her forearms makes her shake. She has no idea why that area of her body causes this reaction. She is more comfortable with a firm flat touch on her forearm as long as it is quick and not a long resting act.

The majority of the group, regardless of the area of the body, don't like being poked. Michael gave a shudder when explaining how he feels if he can hear and feel someone breathing on the back of his neck.

Most of the group decided that it is not necessarily the area being touched that they don't like but how they are touched. Light and soft touches seem to cause the biggest reaction by a person or an object. A bag or a sleeve from a jacket for example.

Anxiety starts to increase the first time a touch takes place and fight or flight mode seems to be activated. With the second touch, Michael would comment and confront the issue in order to hopefully get it resolved. Others, like Anabella and myself, tend to stay quiet and the anxiety increases until we walk away. The best example given of where this may happen is when travelling on the London Underground system.

Tube journeys can be very difficult during the morning and evening rush hour periods. To mitigate this potentially difficult journey, some, like Michael, do not work the 9-5 hours; they start earlier and leave earlier to avoid the majority of the rush. If a bag is pressed up against you during a packed tube, I for one can ignore it very easily and continue to read my book. Michael can suffer panic attacks over it which is why he changed his working hours to reduce this possibility.

Question 17: Is it true that an autistic person can be really high one minute and then super low the next?

Usually. The change seems to be driven by a stimulus reaction or a memory recall. This is when you recall something and then live out that moment again in the present. Anabella explained that while watching a TV show with her grandparents, a scene brought back emotions from a time when she fell out with her friend and that TV show had been on at the time. She ended up crying and replaying the event emotionally years later; it felt so real to her. Her grandparents didn't understand why she was crying at the time.

The highs are called 'funny five minutes' for some. It is where they have a crazy moment, normally as a result of over stimulus, and they tend to try and find something to distract them to calm down. Others seem to have a high for hours where they seem to be bouncing off the walls. Others have a high from a reaction or influence to something.

The super lows seem to be triggered by an outside influence, such as a new person to the group. It comes from something which has or hasn't happened which was outside of their control.

Three of the group have ADHD as well as autism and explain that the ADHD side of their brain is an all or nothing animal. It is either full on, engaged and therefore super focused on the task or is so disengaged or unfocused that it is screaming out to the whole world to leave them alone.

Question 18: Why when you make a mistake do you have a meltdown and create such a fuss over nothing?

Because to us, it is huge. Sally explains that if she has made a social faux pas then she feels that she should know better. The majority of the group explain that they concentrate so hard to try and follow social rules and to interact and behave appropriately, when they make a mistake it feels like the end of the world. All the hard work that they have done so far is gone and they know they should not have made that mistake.

The way the group explain that they have probably set themselves a highly unrealistic expectation of themselves. They seem to set themselves up for failure and are very hard on themselves when that happens. It also appears that they clearly over analyse themselves and the situation around them after every event.

Question 19: Why can you not follow an instruction straight away?

It may depend on the current social interaction that is taking place or it may simply be that they get easily distracted and forget. Sally works for a large international bank. As she works, she wears headphones to reduce distractions and noise, allowing her to focus on work. If someone comes to her bank of desks, she will see them but not register that they maybe there to speak to her. She will carry on working and act like the person is not there, even if she is the only person at her desk out of the team.

The processing part of her brain does not do anything until either the person interacts to promote a response, or another member of the team introduces the person to her. She describes it as a 'deer in the headlights' feeling. She knows the idea of introduction and she knows that she should start the interaction, especially if she is the only one there. For whatever reason – she cannot. Not out of any fear or anxiety over saying hello. It is more the social cue of starting an introduction that is missing from her brain.

Michael and Anabella explain that sometimes they are not able to process the instruction as it is unclear or not logical and, therefore, they struggle to see the objective or purpose of it. Sometimes there is simply too much information and they are not sure exactly what they need to do. Some of the information given may be giving context or setting the scene. However, this information is just noise to them. As it does not do anything to complete the task that they were instructed to do, it is deemed irrelevant. I spend a lot of time filtering out 'noise' from my projects and explaining to people that the background scene setting and information, for the most part, is not relevant.

The difficulty with either of the two things above is explaining to someone that the instruction they have been given is not understood. The group react differently to these situations. Half of the group explain that they are processing the instruction but the facial expressions they show are not thinking expressions. The expressions look like they are bored and not interested. They are looking away and nodding or shaking their head trying to process the instruction internally. The person is still talking but they are giving no response. The person giving the instruction gets frustrated and feels that the autistic person is not listening. Therefore, they are not willing to help when questions are asked after the instructions have been processed.

The other half of the group explain that they respond automatically to the social cues that they have been taught. They acknowledge that someone is giving them an instruction by nodding and looking at the person as much as possible. They say 'yes' at every opportunity to confirm that they have heard and show that they understand (even if they have not understood). Once the conversation is over, they are still processing the instruction. Then feel that they it is too late to ask questions.

Neither of the above helps anyone. The autistic person who wants to do the job, wants to do it as well as possible. They don't want others to feel that they are either not interested or saying yes when they don't understand. It would help if both parties were more self-aware and could create an honest, open space for dialogue with each other. Teachers did not get frustrated with you at primary school when you were struggling with maths. You were shown different ways to tackle the problem or given more time. The same approaches should be followed when you are an adult.

Question 20: How do you feel when you are asked or made to do things which are uncomfortable?

As children most remember reacting and 'kicking off', resulting in arguments and refusing to do something. As an adult, it is easier to avoid things which make them uncomfortable.

Most of the time during their childhood, they were unable to explain what was making them uncomfortable and therefore they reacted in the only way they knew which was deemed as unacceptable social behaviour by others. Anabella goes back to her not being able to hold hands. She could never explain why she could not hold someone's hand, no matter who it was. So, when she was made to do so, she let go and moved away from the person. She did not register or care that there was a road with cars nearby. She did not process that it was dangerous. All she could process was that holding hands was uncomfortable and therefore she needed to get away.

As an adult, you are expected to explain your decisions and there is an expectation that the explanation will be reasonable. This is a difficult area as what is reasonable to one person on the autistic spectrum is not always reasonable for a neuro-typical person, or even another autistic person.

Michael finds it very difficult travelling during rush hour for a number of reasons so starts work at 8:30 and finishes at 4:30. Due to this, he declines any work meetings after 4:30 or any meetings that would not finish before his home time. He just declines the meeting without any explanation.

He has received some challenges over declining meetings. When he explains that these meetings are outside of his working hours, it is sometimes suggested that he may need to work outside his hours to progress through the company. The culture, which I know very well, is one where a lot of people do not follow the working 9-5 pattern, regardless of any contractual obligations.

He has found that once the reason has been explained with regard to his autism and the travelling issue, then the meetings are moved or managed without him. However, he needs to be prompted for that 'reasonable' response, as it is not automatic for him. I would challenge why anyone needs to justify this, regardless of any disability.

Question 21: Do you have any strange traits that you do when you are anxious?

"Traits – yes. Strange traits – I don't think so. But other people seem to think they are strange." Anabella gives this is the initial response with a shrug of her shoulders. She shakes her head slightly when trying to work out why people think these are strange traits.

Sally places her thumbs inside her clenched fists. She likes the feeling of her fingers against her thumbs. She makes lots of facial expressions, not any specific ones, more just moving the muscles within her face as she processes information or her surroundings. She also bites her fingernails down to the bone, as does Anabella and two other members of the group.

Some of these traits have only been identified recently. One of the group is a mentor to autistic children and one child that he was mentoring were obsessed with washing their hands before any activity. During primary school, the child would wash their hands after an English lesson before they started their maths lesson. He worked with the child, school, and parents to help them break down this learnt behaviour and literal reasoning. As a result, he has identified that he himself washes his hands a lot more when changing activities.

Sally explains that she struggles to identify some of her so called 'stranger' traits until it is too late; once she realises, then she has to remove herself from the situation straight away. Such things as subtle movements when she gets anxious – she will rock in her chair or tap her fingers or hide them in her clenched fists and squeeze tighter. However, sometimes the anxiety is so overwhelming that the tapping gets faster and harder or the rocking movements are no longer subtle. It is at this point that others notice. Once others notice, then she feels that her unacceptable social behaviour is there for all to see. That makes her anxiety go into overdrive and she needs to remove herself immediately. She gets up and walks off; it does not matter if she is in a meeting, on the phone or even in the middle of a discussion with someone else. She has to leave.

The hard part is explaining the trait and her reaction to others who are there. One moment Sally is sitting at her desk working, next she is clapping and rocking. Then others notice, she feels all eyes on her and abruptly leaves. This can happen in a relatively short period of time. The reason for it? Unknown. She comes back to her desk and they ask if she is OK and what was wrong. She says she is fine, and nothing is wrong. She cannot explain to others and wants the event forgotten. She places her headphones back on, ignores the attention she is getting and carries on working. She understands that others want to know what happened, but keep being asked will just bring the anxiety back. More importantly, she doesn't know why it happened and therefore cannot tell them.

Question 22: Do you have a good memory and how do you retrieve information you want to recall?

A good memory – more a weird memory than a good one. Sally and Anabella hear a song and they try and remember where they first heard it. They do that by trying to picture the situation or environment that they were in at the time when the song was played. For example, a song from a music lesson at school. They have to picture which music classroom, which teacher, where she was sitting.

Sally says that her memory is nearly non-existent during a conversation if the subject does not interest her or she finds it especially difficult to follow. As a result, she forgets the conversation completely, almost instantly, and does not even believe that it took place at all. She recalls multiple times when her friends have had to remind her that a conversation has taken place, but she is adamant that it hasn't.

Most of the group say that they lost countless things when they were a child. Some still lose things on a regular basis. However, now they try and be more careful with key items, such as phones, keys, and important things. They still forget if they are not in the place that they should be in and they then have to picture the object in their head to recall where it could be. They talk to themselves to concentrate and replay the event in their mind, just like a video – rewind and replay. Some explain that they do not focus on the specific object they have lost; instead, they picture the surrounding objects. An example given by Sally was when she lost her phone. She focused on her purse and remembered that the purse went from the bedroom to the kitchen and then to the spare room as she changed her purse for a night out with her friends. She found her phone with her old purse in the spare room where she left it.

Anabella recalls at secondary school that she had a key list of ten things that she needed to do every morning. This list was stuck to the back of the bedroom door, with the same list on the kitchen cabinet. This ensured that it was visible for her in the two key places she goes into every morning. This helped her do those tasks every day. She still has this list now.

Others recall adverts, random information, and useless facts which they heard once and then forever remember. Michael explained that it took over two years to learn and remember his partner's birthday and even now he still needs to check when it is. Others have created specific places for things and say that it may have created some OCD tendencies.

I, myself, replay things in my head like a video. One thing that I always seem to do is on a Monday morning is replay my Thursday evening from when I got home from work, as I work from home on a Friday. When I walk through the front door, where I placed my work bag, where I placed my suit and then hit pause when I see my work pass and then get it before I leave the house.

Question 23: Are you under or over sensitive to noise?

The biggest triggers for the group seem to be noise, followed closely by touch. Sometimes it could be just an additional piece of noise that tips them over the edge. A lot of the group explain that on a standard day, they hear so much around them, lots of background noise which they are unable to filter out. Background noise such as the clicking of a mouse, the tapping of a keyboard, colleagues talking on the phone, even others walking around. All of these noises can be heard clearly, some louder than others, but all of them clearly audible. The group explain that they have to concentrate so hard to try and tune in and out of the different noises depending on what is going on.

Imagine, if you can, that you are walking through a large shopping centre. You hear everyone near you walking, the clip-clop sound of a hundred pairs of shoes and trainers on the tiled floor. The people are talking, some loud and laughing, others quiet, almost whispering. Music is being played in Topshop and Primark, loud enough for you to hear as you are walking past. The tannoy system is asking for the manager to come to the ground check out. The security guard is messaging a colleague on his walkie-talkie. The people who accidently bumped into you saying sorry as well as your own voice saying sorry or excuse me as you manoeuvre your way through the store.

That is what the group explain that they can hear all the time. They can hear all those noises and if they focus and concentrate, they can hear them all very clearly and distinctly. However, it is mentally draining when they try to focus in and out all the time. The group explain that they have to keep filtering the noise so that they are listening and responding when having a conversation with someone.

In a work setting, the noises are replaced with the humming of computers on every desk; the printers; people talking on the phone or within their teams; the tapping of fingers on keyboards. The tapping can be very light, very heavy, very slow or extremely fast. Sitting in an open plan office with nearly forty people all typing is just a sea of noise. Then the chairs move and people walk around.

Question 24: Why do you always fidget? Do you have a problem remaining still?

Some of the group have ADHD as well as being autistic. They explain that they are not sure if it is the ADHD or autism that makes them fidget or a mixture of both, but they seem to be constantly moving. Sally explains that she has to shift around a bit. Even if it is in her chair and just shifts her position every ten–twenty seconds. It seems to be a need. She says that her brain is always working at 200%. While she is processing, her body needs to do something as well – this is the explanation for her fidgeting – tap on the table, play an imaginary piano, tap her feet, move her head, spin a pen around her fingers. Anything and everything that is minor, mostly subtle, and mostly subconsciously. She does not mean to distract or annoy others, especially at work, but sometimes others around her comment that she is tapping and distracting them.

Most of the group struggle to remain still unless they are fully involved with something. The only activity that results in remaining still is reading. The group love reading, drifting off into a far-away land and losing themselves in their book. This results in a very calm and stationary state where movement is rare to non-existent.

Question 25: Why do you do things differently to others?

We don't have a choice. It is how we interpret things. When something happens, we see it differently; sometimes we do not process, understand, or express the same as a neurotypical person and therefore we can't do it the same.

We learn a way that works for us; each one of us are different and what works for one autistic person may not work for another. Anabella compares it to how she was taught maths at primary school. She was taught three different ways to do additions, subtractions, and multiplications. She remembers that she struggled with two of these methods and generally the third was the best for her, although she still found it hard.

Her parents taught her the way they were taught at school – which is now called the column method. You focus on each column, one under each other.

```
    Th  H  T  U         Th   H    T   U
     4  5  5  2          3  ⁶7̶  ¹1   8
 +   3  5  6  9     -    1   2    4   2
     8  1  2  1          2   4    7   6
        1  1  1
```

Now she does her own method for any maths problem that she gets challenged with and this approach works for her. She remembers that her teachers told her that she had to complete certain tasks with the other method that she did not fully understand. When she did the above, she got the right answer but did not get the mark because she did the incorrect method. Welcome to the world of our lovely education curriculum. She says that she gets told to solve other problems or behave a certain way. She feels more comfortable doing it her way, which is socially acceptable and no one has any issues with it, but a teacher says you must do this way only. How counter-intuitive for our future generations and in life. During my role working for a bank in HR Reward, which requires lots of mathematical problems, I am not told which method to use to work out the sum. I am asked to work out the answer and ensure that it is correct.

Others explain that they learnt a 'safe way' to do things which worked for them and therefore they have no reason to change it. If the method requires changing, then it must be brought to them by one of their few 'safe' friends who allow them to try new things and not get upset if they break socially acceptable protocol. This is the best way to engage in social interactions and build awareness and tolerance.

Sally explained that she has to process her moments of madness. She must wait for the situation to end, however long that may be, then try and explain and show the person what she sees. This is not very easy as what she sees as 'normal' she finds difficult to find words for. She is unable to explain in simple clear statements that a neurotypical person would understand. She has to use the words or phrases in her head which make perfect sense to her, but normally not for others.

Question 26: Does your over/under sensitivity to noise affect other areas such as pain?

The majority of the group feel that it does not turn into an actual physical pain, but because the sensitivity is so personally internalised, it feels painful. If you are feeling tired or sad, then it feels even worse.

Sally explains that because she has to work so hard every second of every day to mask her behaviour, when she is in actual pain then this is the one area which she cannot mask. When in pain, her masking ability disappears.

Question 27: Why are you extremely picky over food and drink?

There is no real consensus from the group on this question. While I have been working in Canary Wharf, I have generally had the same thing for lunch, from the same shop for nearly twelve years. Others, such as Michael or Sally are willing to try new things in certain situations. Sally explains that as long as the things that she does not like are not present in the ingredients for the meal that is being cooked, then she is willing to try something new. However, she is equally happy to eat the same thing every night because she likes it.

    Others explained that they really enjoy food and will to try anything and everything possible, regardless of what it is. This is not your typical autistic behaviour. The only issue that they see when trying something new is that they may not feel full or satisfied afterwards.

Question 28: Are you always very anxious and worry about every single thing?

Sally nodded emphatically and screamed out that she is generally anxious and worries about everything, all of the time. She worries and is anxious from the moment she closes her front door in the morning heading to work until she walks back through her front door and into the safe area of her own house. Once there, she does not need to worry about anything anymore from the outside world. However, it is not always her safe place as it should be.

Rules, structure, and routine help to keep the anxiety away. One example of this is when she lost some tickets for a show she was going to. She was so anxious that she spent hours in her house searching: she upended most of her bedroom, then the living room and other rooms, including the kitchen. This started at 1 a.m. and she finally found them around 4 a.m.

She was anxious throughout until she found them and then she was calmer and happy. She had found the tickets and knew where they were. She placed them in a different place and felt she could relax now. The fact that the tickets were for a show that was not for another few months was irrelevant to her. She was unable to sleep knowing that the tickets were lost; she could not forget about them until the next morning or leave it until another day to search. She had to search and find them that night, at that time. Once they were found, she could go back to sleep, even if it were only going to be for a few hours.

Question 29: Isn't there any medication you can take to stop being autistic most of the time?

The members of the group which answered this question all reacted in the same way before answering. They all looked fed up and rolled their eyes, even at me. One of the most common misunderstandings or typical questions an autistic person seems to be asked about is whether medicine or growing up removes autism.

Only Sally takes medicine for autism. She explained that there is some medicine which can help control some of the uncomfortable feelings that an autistic person experiences. A doctor explained what happens with Anabella's ADHD medicine. The doctor said that just because on the outside Anabella is calmer, the ADHD madness that she is experiencing inside her head is still going on. It is still going on at the same rate as it was before. The difference? I just can't see it.

We need to make society understand that autism is not a condition for which you can take a pill and stop being autistic.

Question 30: Do you think your ADHD is more manageable with medicine?

For those in the group who have ADHD as well as autism, they agreed that yes, it was so much more manageable. Sally has been on drugs for her ADHD from the age of fifteen until twenty-one. She took Ritalin for a period of 6–9 months, but it was not the best drug for her. She changed to Dexamphetamine which she took for nearly six years. She is adamant that without that drug, she would not have got an education at all. She would not have been able to sit GCSEs, let alone get her A-levels and her university degree. She said that the drug opened up that part of her brain which was fighting to retain information and allow her to fully focus.

She tried to process the information without the drug. However, due to sensory overload from her surroundings, she was unable to focus and got easily distracted. This medicine helped her focus. She says from her own experience that parents, as well as teachers, need to be educated and understand the difference between a child pushing boundaries and learning and believing that drugging up is the answer. Blaming the ADHD as the only reason that they have not learnt something.

As with anything, there is normally a negative side. Everything works in a balance and Sally found a massive negative side effect which resulted in her choosing to come off the drug. That side effect, in Sally's case, was dependency. The last two years of the drug were the hardest. However, this was not a planned situation. She went to Thailand to travel and ended up working there for a while. Her drug was illegal in Thailand so she had to have a different one instead. The change of medication impacted her state of mind severely during the day. It had such a massive impact that she felt that she could not focus without the drug.

It was like torture to know that she was not fully in control of herself. She had worked so hard on having control of and masking those traits which seem to be socially unacceptable, and then years later those feelings being brought back but a hundred times worse. She worked as hard as she has ever worked before to regain control and she was able to learn new strategies and techniques without Dexamphetamine.

It gave her the ability to be able to manage herself better. She is grateful now and although it was hard, it was worth it. She says she would not go back on drugs now. She recognises that at fifteen, she was not mature enough to manage without them. At that time, she needed them, and they served her well. Now she does not need them.

Question 31: Do you think that your secondary school / university kept you focused enough you stop your disruptive behaviour?

"Not a chance. It was the drugs that were the key thing which kept me focused," replied Sally. Support was available from the school, but the support did not keep her focused alone. The members of the group who had taken drugs all explained that they needed both to get through the education system.

Three of this group have ADHD as well. They explained that the drugs were key, especially as ADHD is a very public thing that everyone can see. Autism, they feel, is more private and less visible until it is too late.

Question 32: Is there anything that you constantly struggle with, that you feel that you should not struggle with?

The group struggle with a number of things that they feel that they should not struggle with. Sally explained that she feels tired all the time. This is her biggest struggle and she would like to feel better about this. However, the reason for her being so tired is because of the extreme levels of concentration that she has to use to function. She feels that she has to be at 200% all the time with no down time during the day.

Others in the group explain that anything socially is a struggle. Doing a social faux pas is the most embarrassing thing. They understand society's rules, most of the time, and when they forget them then they struggle heavily to recover.

Question 33: Why do you interrupt when others are talking?

Because they want to join in, and they are super excited about the subject being discussed. They want to know what the others know and are so excited that they blurt things out. Autistic people want to be a part of everything; they are interested in others and friends. They try not to turn the conversation into being about themselves but somehow their brain does that and as a result they end up making comments which others interpret as making the conversation about them.

Due to this, they get called selfish. This is one of the hardest insults that some of these members can take. They are not selfish; they want to help others, talk to others, and are interested in others. The problem is that the autism is at the centre of everything for this group.

Question 34: Do you think that your behaviour can be inappropriate?

Yes – it can be. Mainly because I am reacting to certain things which are overwhelming for me. The behaviour is not appropriate, as per society's standards, at the time in the situation. For the group, they behave as per the situation, which is exactly the same as a neurotypical person. Sally explained that she was having a really bad ADHD day at work. She was bouncing off the walls, fidgeting more than usual and to the outside world it could have been seen as very childish behaviour. She could also be aggressive to her team members. She understands why it is inappropriate.

The issue is, at the time, perfectly simple. The brain does not send signals explaining that how they are reacting is inappropriate. Tapping on the table is one method Sally uses to calm down and therefore, it is performed. However, it can be very distracting for others in the team and this is why it is deemed inappropriate.

Manners are also a very big thing for the group. Anabella explains that her family dynamic is very heavy on manners and being kind – say please, thank you, excuse me, shoes off at the front door, say sorry. Sally says her household was the same as Anabella's. Now Sally says that as a young adult, she appreciates the importance of good manners and if people do not have them, then she does not want to associate with them.

I remember that I felt that I had to apologise for everything that I did. 'Sorry' became the most used word for me and others growing up at school, progressing through work and into adult life. A reaction, a comment. Anything that I seemed to do, I upset someone, somehow and automatically 'sorry' was said, even when I did not know what I had done.

As I have grown up, I have matured and tried to work out why I get certain reactions. Some I can understand, and I try to change and improve from those experiences and situations. Others, I still see no issues with what I have either said or done. I put it down to the other person and their interpretation of the situation. Everyone should look at things and see if it is their fault or not and behave appropriately.

Question 35: How do you feel when someone tells you that you are being inappropriate?

There were different reactions to this question, but the majority of the group react with the fight or flight mode when this happens to them.

Some of the group respond very aggressively and then shut down completely. They react this way because they are trying so extremely hard not to be inappropriate that when they are told the opposite then they feel like a child again when they were what seemed to be constantly scorned. They believe that they are doing really well and then to be told that they are not is very upsetting. They get angry, all their belief falls away and they want to defend themselves; they shut down after the initial shock and reaction. Part of the shutdown means not listening to anyone, not interacting, and remaining silent and unresponsive.

The other half of the group go into flight mode. They do not react angrily or get aggressive; they do the opposite. They shrink into themselves before shutting down, like the others. They leave the situation altogether. Some just walk off; others have been known to actually run away and break down on the way to a safe place. This is not restricted to being outside, it could happen in the house with family and the safe place would be another room.

They have the same reaction when in their safe place; they remain silent and unresponsive with others if they are there. They replay the event in their heads all evening, the next day and sometimes for even longer, replaying what they said, how the person reacted – over analysing every minute detail to try and understand what they did wrong and how not to do it again.

Question 36: How are you finding secondary school / university?

Only Anabella from the group is in education. She finds she has more freedom than she had in primary school, which is good. Year 7 was difficult as it was a new environment and she was scared of getting in trouble. She wasn't sure of how to act and behave in a new setting. Now she is year 9, she has just selected her GCSE options and is looking forward to starting her GCSEs in year 10 from September 2020. The environment is more relaxed.

Anabella struggled to explain how she finds a typical day and how her condition impacts her during her day. She just sees it as a place that she needs to go to learn. She has good teachers and not so good teachers, in part because of her interest in the subject and in part due to the other children. She is struggling to understand that she has only two years left there. By July 2022 she will have taken her GCSEs and then school will be over. She is unsure what happens next.

Question 37: Can you describe what you see and feel when you get anxious?

Michael and Sally explained that they see the world like a pulse setting on disco lights. It shines bright and then gets dimmer. It is a flash but generally only certain things that they see are pulsing. Maybe the objects on the table are pulsing or the area in which the loud noises are coming from.

Breathing becomes harder; it starts to be short sharp bursts instead of long slow deep breaths which are controlled. Sally says her cheeks get hot, hot enough to touch. They start glowing red and her heart seems to start racing, like there is a race between her lungs and heart as to which can be the quickest.

Question 38: Why do you find it difficult to hold someone's hand?

"Because I don't like it," said Anabella. A good answer and a perfectly acceptable one. Just because you do not understand it, or cannot relate to it, does not make it any less valid. The reasons why some of the group do not like it are slightly different.

Sally says that she can get clammy hands. She becomes subconscious about it and so avoids holding hands with anyone. She can hold hands with people that she knows very well. She would rather link arms than hold hands. She prefers to be linked at the elbow joint so that there is no skin-to-skin touching, but still gets that safe feeling from being close to someone. Touching over clothes is not an issue for her; it is the skin-to-skin touching that causes her issue.

Anabella will only hold my hand and no one else's. It took years before she was comfortable doing that. She started by holding my jacket pocket instead. When she was younger, she would hold the pocket of my hoodie when crossing roads or a strap from my bag when we walked to school. All of this allowed her to feel close to me but not actually touch me.

What about if you liked someone? Would you seek out their hand?

Some of them explained that they would but the idea of doing it makes them a little anxious. Sally said she would have to build herself up to it, maybe even have a few drinks to remove some of her inhibitions first.

Question 39: Is it true that the mental health of an autistic person is more up and down than a non-autistic person?

The group believe that this could potentially be true. Most of the group, myself included, feel that our mental health is a very fast rollercoaster ride. Some days are better than others. Sometimes they can be OK for a day and then feel very low for weeks on end. They often have the feeling of not knowing why they are so low.

They can see the difference with their non-autistic friends and family members and their perception and disclosure of issues such as the sensory challenges that they face as well as periods of anxiety. Part of the group are envious of how non-autistic people seem to manage it and try and look at it from a non-autistic way. However, it makes even less sense to them. Maybe those non-autistic people are struggling as much as we are, we just can't see it.

Anabella explained that she found listening to a non-autistic person explain how they see and deal with their mental health issues the same as her reading an instruction manual in Spanish, but she only speaks French. She can see some words and has an idea, as some Spanish and French are similar, but then finds out that the French and Spanish word do not mean the same thing.

I feel that there needs to be more research into the relationship between mental health and autism to establish whether there is indeed a link as we believe.

Question 40: What has helped you with your mental wellbeing?

Having a safe place. Sally lives in London and having the escape of going home helps her. It is a place where she can be herself and not have to mask her behaviours as often. She also notices now when her mental wellbeing is slipping and actively seeks out therapy sessions. She did not have a great support network during school or university, and she has been doing this pretty much all on her own. She feels that for the last ten years she has been coping more by luck than by actually managing it with specific techniques or strategies.

One thing that she feels helped her is that there was an end to the situation. For school, her aim was getting her GCSEs; at sixteen it was going to end, regardless. She just had to get through the next few years. University was the same; she had an end period and end date.

I firmly believe that a number of issues with society could be reduced by people learning how to self-care, including with their mental health. This would require it to be taught at primary and secondary schools. Once you leave, you are aware of yourself better. You are able to recognise when you need a break, when you are slipping and need to reach out for help. Sadly, it would be something else for our education system which is already overflowing.

Question 41: Do you struggle getting ready in the morning?

It seems that the morning routine is key for a lot of the group, including myself. If the morning goes well that it is a good start to the day; if not, then the whole day could be a struggle.

Some find the morning difficult regardless and can easily get distracted. Anabella explains that she always gets distracted by something and loses focus. If it is a short distraction like five to fifteen minutes, then she is OK and it does not generally disrupt her day. Any longer than fifteen minutes then she feels that she has wasted time. She is extremely hard on herself and can feel like a failure all day.

Sally agrees with Anabella and says that sometimes she has lost focus for potentially an hour in the mornings and it ruins her day as she cannot let that go.

Question 42: Do you understand the concept of time?

I do not understand the concept of time when it comes to memory and recalling events. I forget the order of things and when something took place in relation to something else. I can remember the event in great detail, but not the timing around it.

It seems that a lot of the group are the same as me, not fully understanding the concept of time. They think that they have twenty minutes to do something and then all of a sudden, they have two minutes left and they do not realise where the time has gone.

Others have a very good internal clock and understand how much time they have to do things. They may need to be reminded of the task, but they know the timeframe. If asked to do something within fifteen minutes, then they will do it.

Question 43: It is reported that autistic people suffer from sleep disorders, do you?

Sally and I have trouble sleeping a lot. However, this is usually because of an incident that has taken place earlier that day and we are either trying to process it or are replaying the event over and over in our heads.

Sally loves sleep and says that the medication she was on was the cause of her insomnia. When things get too much, sleep is one of her escapes. She has very vivid dreams and she feels that these can be highly addictive, so she enjoys them. She feels completely safe and has no need to worry about masking her behaviours and worrying about others while she is sleeping.

Question 44: Why do you tap your hands and bite your fingernails all the time?

"The tapping of fingers is a calming mechanism used when I am feeling stressed or anxious," replied both Sally and me. Sometimes it is because we are really engaged with a task. We both love music and love to lose ourselves inside the music, especially classical piano music for me (as I am learning the piano and can play a few pieces). I catch myself at work, while listening to a piece, and end up playing the song on my desk like a piano. Luckily, my colleagues are aware of this behaviour and no longer look at me strangely.

Two of the group explained that they used to bite their fingernails. Anabella once bit the complete fingernail off and it took over five months to grow back. Sally used to cover her fingernails with a special nail polish which eventually stopped her from eating them. It was very common for her to eat or bite her nails when she was anxious and when those levels increased then she would bite them even more.

Question 45: Why do you always line up toys / items and put them in colour / size order?

Not all of the group do this. However, they do like to have things in a set place or set position. For example, Anabella arranges her collection of snow globes in a particular order, from the first one she was given to the most recent one. She cannot have them in different places. The special ones have pride of place in the collection.

When Sally has her friends over, as much as she loves them and enjoys seeing them, she is ready for them to leave after three or four hours. If they move things around the house, this raises her anxiety levels. Sally is happy to share things; it is the issue of having things moved from the places she needs them to be which is stressful for her.

Anabella and I are always lining things up, using different categories such as colour or size. It could be coins, for example. If I have change, I will re-arrange it into size order and place it back in my pocket. Anytime I get coins out, I repeat the order process before placing them back in my pocket. It is not an OCD thing; it is my brain saying that the coins should be in order or I can't function. Anabella has her clothes set up in her wardrobe ranging from dark colours to light with every shade in between. She explains that sometimes the order of something is calming her down. It reduces her anxiety of finding something she wants to wear or is specifically searching for.

Question 46: Do you seem to remember and repeat slogans and catchphrases easily?

The group all admit to remembering all sorts of random things, from songs to TV shows and even recite an entire episode of Red Dwarf or 'Allo 'Allo, for example. Others just remember random facts that they have heard and need to repeat them when something triggers that memory.

I sometimes get a song stuck in my head and I have to repeat it over and over and over again. No other song. Sometimes I sing it (badly, as my kids will confirm) or I find it on YouTube and play it on repeat. Just that one song. Sally explained that she found a new song while searching YouTube and fell in love with it so much that she played the same song repeatedly for four hours straight.

Question 47: You seem to be able to repeat lines in TV shows. Can you repeat whole episodes?

Oh yes, explained four of the group. I brought my kids up watching lots of old 1990s BBC comedy shows which is helpful now as anytime the family need something easy to watch then these shows are top of the list. The whole family can almost repeat whole episodes. One time, Anabella wanted to test herself to see if she did know the script as well as she thought she did. She watched two episodes of Red Dwarf on mute and just spoke the words of the different characters. There were a few sentences that were not exactly right but it was close enough.

Sally explained that she does remember films and shows but is not very good at remembering any key lines. However, she does have a good memory for the numbering system that is used. Based on the series and episode number, she can tell you what the episode is called and what it is about.

Question 48: Do you like reading or do you struggle with the understanding / context of the written piece?

The group love reading. Michael, Sally and Anabella loved reading from a young age and understood the context very well. Others hated reading when they were younger and struggled in school, like me. I had difficulty understanding the context of some pieces and what they meant. Written work was never an issue but the instructions were hard to process.

This could be because the instructions were complex or had multiple parts. They could only remember the first one or two and then they were not sure what to do next. Sometimes it is actually something very simple that proves tricky; something that ten minutes later they fully understand but struggled to process immediately.

Question 49: Why do you get distracted so easily and so often?

If we knew the answer to this, we wouldn't get distracted anymore.

We concentrate extremely hard and being told to concentrate more is soul destroying. Our brains are processing everything that we can see, hear, and feel and we have to work hard to tune out all the additional noise in order to focus on what is happening. We are trying not to get distracted by the other thirty-odd things that our brains are noticing as clearly as that one instruction that we are receiving.

Everyone has bad days, and, for whatever reason, may not be working to the best of their ability. We are no different. We get tired as well; we get distracted and forget things maybe more than a non-autistic person. But it is not helpful to comment on the things we forget and believe we are not trying because you remember the instruction and we got distracted.

Question 50: Why do you keep running off?

I do this because I am either excited and want to get where I am going as quickly as possible or I need to get away from a situation.

It may be that some people don't run but march off somewhere quickly. They usually have had a conversation in their head, know what they are going to do next and head off in anticipation. For example, being out with friends for the evening and knowing the next place is a bar or restaurant, so they head off first. The issue is usually that they have not had the conversation with the rest of the group of friends who, therefore, become confused and wonder why they are walking off, assuming that they are upset. It throws the dynamic of the evening out. They may now feel isolated and not want to continue with the night out.

Question 51: Repetition is a key trait for an autistic person. What do you repeat over and over again?

Routine. Routine. Routine.

The most repetitive thing that is done is the routine that each person has. Some break their day into sections and then sub-routines. The reason behind this is that it breaks tasks into smaller manageable pieces. When things are broken down it provides security and safety and, for some, there is an end to the task or section. If something is making them anxious then they have an end position to aim for. They know at some point it will end and they can rest and take a breather if needed, before moving onto the next stage or task.

Anabella explained that because the world is such a big random place and she tends to struggle within it, that her own routine is something that she can fall back on when something new appears or changes which she has no control over.

Question 52: Do you need cues or prompts to do things or be reminded of the task you have been set?

Yes, we are very forgetful and often need lots of prompts to keep us on task. Most of the time, the prompts are helpful. However, it can be frustrating if the reminders are too frequent or, more commonly, if they are very harsh. Being too harsh gives the impression that people are becoming frustrated, and this can trigger anxiety issues.

Sally explained that sometimes she may be halfway through a task with a plan in her head for the next steps. Then she is given a reminder and this causes her to forget the process she has just worked out. She then has to start again. Sometimes she even questions what she did before, believing that she had misunderstood the original instruction. The previous five to ten minutes becomes blank. She has no idea what she has said or what has been said to her when given an instruction.

Anabella explains that it feels like she has short-term memory loss. Anything that was given to Anabella as an instruction within the last hour, sometimes even less, then she would generally forget very easily until she was reminded.

Question 53: Why do you have trouble remaining still, regardless of the situation?

The older members explain that this is easier now that they are working but during school and their teenage years it was difficult. It was not until their early to mid-twenties that it started to settle down and they were able to manage it slightly better.

Anabella and Sally explained that they need to shift their position and potentially move at least three or four times an hour. Others, however, could not sit still for more than two minutes. From shifting position in a chair, to tapping the table with fingers, clapping, or doing anything that requires the movement of arms, legs, and head.

The most uncontrollable place for most was in primary school and into secondary school. The issue was that teachers seemed to want the children to sit extremely still, which was not possible and, logically, served no purpose to the child. As long as others were not being disturbed then this should not have been an issue. If they did not realise that it was distracting for others, then the instruction to sit still was illogical to them. The group all understand the reason why children cannot just get up when they want but they feel that someone lightly tapping on a table or wriggling their fingers was made into a bigger issue by teachers or adults. The other children in class, did not seem to notice or mind.

I can relate to both Anabella and my middle daughter, Lucia, and their classes. Both have conditions which cause them to behave in different ways to their peers. Lucia's class did not mind the brace that she wore or some of the things she did. It was the same with Anabella and her fidget toys. When they were first introduced the other children noticed, but it soon became normal that Anabella played with a soft blue tear-shaped toy while writing. After that – no distractions and no issues.

Other adult members of the group explain that they are always moving. I, myself, walk around my desk while on the phone and tap the desk lightly. I have even been known to sit on the floor against the window during calls in an open-plan office. No one says anything. People who do not know me, look at me the first few times but in general, ignore it. After that, as long as it is not disturbing them or getting in anyone else's way then there is no harm. I have only had one person in over ten years tell me that I was disturbing them and I stopped. When that person was around, I focused hard not to do the trait which disturbed them by doing different activities to calm myself down.

Question 54: Is your brain consistently working fast?

For the majority of the group and for the majority of the time, yes. Our brains are working at what seems to be 200 mph for 80–90% of the time.

The other 10–20% of the time, they could be completely blank. This feels quite scary as there seems to be nothing there at all. Like a TV screen when you turn it off – nothing but pure blankness.

After working at such a high speed for so long, the brain then shuts down. It is like a reset button; it is unable to focus anymore, even on the simplest task. On those occasions during this recharge time, they tend to be on their own and just sit there doing nothing, waiting for their brain to reboot.

This is one of the most common reasons why the members of the group require some alone time every day, even if it is just for five minutes. Or perhaps half an hour every few days whereby the brain can reboot.

Question 55: Do you have a detailed timetable for every day and every hour within the day?

This method worked during school because there were so many extra activities that had to be remembered and be prepared for. However, most of the group do not have this anymore.

They explain that they break down days into smaller, more manageable sections. A day could be split into the following: morning, work, evening, etc. Some break down their days into smaller sections such as: morning, breakfast, travel to work, work, break, lunch, gym, dinner, travel home, free time and bed. Individuals use whatever works for them.

Conclusion:

This was a project which grew and grew the more we discussed differences to each other, to mainstream society, and especially the media and the images they use of an autistic person. However, the group are not that different to any other group that you see. Imagine you go for Sunday lunch on a warm summer's day. You will see many different groups of people out and about. You see young couples together; families and children with or without dogs, just relaxing; the group who went out partying the night before and now just want sleep or go home. Now look at each person in that group. Each one is different. You will have your loud personalities and ones that you get drawn to who have a presence. You have the quiet ones who hang back. You have the ones always making jokes and maybe one who always wants to be the centre of attention. The fact is the group enjoy each other but will have a problem at some point. Some may be not following the joke and need to have it explained, for example. An autistic person is no different. They are a part of that group no less than any other person. You have those who want to be the centre of attention. Those who sit in the background but then come to the forefront once in a while. Others who are always making jokes, about others or themselves. Those who never seem to get the joke.

This group struggles with things like everyone else does at times. They struggle more socially than others; they see things differently and interpret things differently to others. They struggle to articulate what they see differently and how it is different to a neurotypical person. The main and most simple reason for this is that they are not neurotypical. They do not understand how a neurotypical person may see things and just as a neurotypical person cannot see as an autistic person does.

That is why communication is key. It is not just about raising awareness over autism and any other important issue taking place in the world. The point is to develop and change awareness to acceptance. Autism is not going to go away. It is part of a person. It is part of their DNA. Autism is a part of our society. You can no more learn to stop being autistic than you can changing your eye colour from brown to blue.

This group have had very different upbringings and have gone through different situations, but the biggest thing is this group does not give up. It is hard and they struggle; they have some really bad days at some points. Every person wants to be accepted for who they are. You do not have to like every person, autistic or not. However, an autistic person should not be disliked purely because they are autistic.

Meeting new people can be scary for anyone. Some people you seem to click with straight away, others take a while to warm up and it takes time for you to build a relationship. Others you do not get on with at all as there is no common ground or there could be a clash of personalities. Whatever it is, you do not then go around and say derogatory things about them to everyone you meet.

All people can be misunderstood and with social media, it makes it even easier to misunderstand something. Only 7% of what you say is covered by the actual words you use. The rest is body language and tone which cannot be expressed through a Tweet, a Facebook post, or a message on WhatsApp.

What do we all need to do about this group and any other group?

Be kind. Take your time to understand. Raise awareness of this group and others. Accept that they are different to you and do things differently to you. Everyone makes mistakes, no one is immune to messing up and some mistakes are bigger than others. However, you can learn from your mistakes. You should be held accountable, but not vilified for them. Everyone made mistakes when they were younger; you were taught how to behave, how to act and learnt from that incident. You may have even made that same mistake again, and you tried again. That process does not stop once you become an adult. It does not stop when you get a job. It does not stop when you become a parent yourself or even a grandparent. You develop, you evolve, and you learn, and you teach and most importantly, you live.

Lets all live for a world where acceptance is the next lesson.

ABOUT THE AUTHOR

Dave Russell was born and raised in South London. He now lives in Essex with his family and was diagnosed with autism in 2017. He has worked in the financial services industry for nearly fifteen years within the Human Resources department, specifically performance and deferred reward. He has also been raising awareness for disabilities within the workplace as well as support for those with dependants with disabilities for nearly ten years. In the summer of 2018, he set up his own company (dis)Ability and Inclusion, which specialises in helping companies support their workforce with seminars, interactive discussions or awareness and educational material. He also works closely with schools creating educational material and discussing support available for teachers as well as parents.

Company Website: www.disabilityandinclusion.com

Printed in Great Britain
by Amazon